Published by Oxmoor House, Inc., and Leisure Arts, Inc.

Library of Congress Catalog Number: 84-63030
Hardcover ISBN: 0-8487-1130-0
Softcover ISBN: 0-8487-1161-0
ISNN: 0883-9077
Manufactured in the United States of America
First Printing

Editor-in-Chief: Nancy J. Fitzpatrick
Senior Crafts Editor: Susan Ramey Wright
Senior Editor, Editorial Services: Olivia Kindig Wells
Director of Manufacturing: Jerry Higdon
Art Director: James Boone

Christmas is Coming!

Editor: Linda Baltzell Wright
Editorial Assistant: Shannon Leigh Sexton
Illustrator and Designer: Barbara Ball
Copy Chief: Mary Jean Haddin
Copy Editor: Susan Smith Cheatham
Copy Assistant: Leslee Rester Johnson
Senior Photographer: John O'Hagan
Photostylist: Connie Formby
Production Manager: Rick Litton
Associate Production Manager: Theresa L. Beste
Production Assistant: Marianne Jordan

Contents

Mrs. Santa's Workshop

Children's Workshop: Happy Holiday Crafts

Trimmings to Fix

Presents to Make

Parents' Workshop: Great Gifts for Children

Grin and Wear It

Just for Fun

Designers & Contributors

3

Dear Parents

Preparing for Christmas is serious business with kids. There are ornaments to make, cards to color, and presents to prepare—all the day after Thanksgiving! To keep creativity riding high the entire season, peruse the following pages. Each project in "Children's Workshop" is labeled for difficulty—Level 1 is the easiest and Level 3 the most difficult. Then flip to "Parent's Workshop" for inspiring designs that you can make. Full of ideas, *Christmas is Coming!* will inspire little hands—and big— to create some holiday magic this Christmas.

4

Dear Kids

Have you ever wondered what Mrs. Santa is doing at the North Pole while Santa and his elves are busy making toys? Turn to the first chapter, "Mrs. Santa's Workshop," and you'll discover that she is busy making special toys of her own. She gathers her tools—bowls, spoons, and frosting "glue"—and makes the most delicious toys. Yes, delicious! Her toys are toys you can eat! This year, Mrs. Santa shares some of her own favorite toy recipes. You'll find Santa's Dominoes, North Pole Paint Sets, Stardust Wands, and Peppermint Skates. Even Mrs. Santa's reindeer friends have come up with toy ideas. Prancer invented Peanut Butter Play Dough and Comet made a kaleidoscope that's filled with candy.

But these aren't the only gift ideas in *Christmas is Coming!* In "Presents to Make," you'll find ideas for everybody on your list. There's a Squish 'n Wish for the dreamer you know, Crazy Hats for a sister who likes to dress up, and a bank for your budget-conscious brother.

When it's time to decorate, flip to "Trimmings to Make." It's full of easy-to-do holiday decorations. There are Nutty Reindeer Ornaments, a Spoon Angel, and Glitter Ornaments. You can even make a skirt for your Christmas tree or a cover for your mailbox.

But before you start on any project, be sure to check with a grown-up.

Mrs. Santa's Workshop

In Santa's workshop at the North Pole, you know you'll find Santa and the elves busy making toys for good girls and boys. But there's another workshop you may not have heard about—Mrs. Santa's. She doesn't use hammers and nails and paint like Santa does. Instead, she combines candy and other confections to create special toys—the kind you can eat! With Mrs. Santa's suggestions and simple directions, it will be easy for you to make her delicious candy treats to share with your family and friends this Christmas.

Mrs. Santa's Suggestions

1. Always check with a grown-up before starting a project.

2. Wash your hands before you begin.

3. Read the directions all the way through before starting.

4. Ask a grown-up for help when the directions say to use a knife.

5. Remember to clean up when you are finished.

Mrs. Santa's Christmas Cottage

Home to Mrs. Santa's workshops, this candy cottage is an inviting place to visit. However, if you're not planning a trip to the North Pole this year, you can create your own miniature Christmas cottage. Just look over Mrs. Santa's house plans and grab your apron before you begin.

You will need (for 1 cottage):
A grown-up
Tracing paper
Pencil
Scissors
17" x 30" piece of heavy cardboard
Tape
3 (16-ounce) boxes of sugar cubes
Table knife
4 (16-ounce) cans of ready-to-spread vanilla frosting
4 heavy books
Plastic wrap
5 (4½" x 1") fudge-dipped peanut butter wafer bars

6 (5" x 2¼") unbroken graham crackers
3 dozen powdered sugar-covered butter cookies, cut in half
15 circular roll candies
4 (3½") old-fashioned peppermint sticks
4 (1½") jujube bears
3 (½-ounce) strawberry-flavored chewy fruit rolls
17 sticks of fruit-striped chewing gum
1 candy button
1 (4½-ounce) can of green decorating frosting, with tips
Assorted multicolored nonpariels
6 red cinnamon candies
16 pastel flower candy sprinkles

Making the Cottage

1. Cut a 17″ x 15″ piece of cardboard to use as a base under the cottage. Trace and cut out the end pattern for the cottage. Cut 2 ends. From the remaining cardboard, cut 2 (5″ x 7″) front/back pieces. Tape the pieces together to make the cottage. Stand the cottage in the center of the base.

2. Ask the grown-up to use the knife to cut 10 sugar cubes in half. Use the vanilla frosting as the mortar and line up 13 whole sugar cubes against the front of the cardboard cottage. For the next row, start with a half cube, add 12 whole cubes, and end with another half cube. Continue bricking the walls until they are 11 cubes high. Use the half cubes on the ends of every other row. Brick the wall for the back of the cottage in the same way.

3. Line up 9 sugar cubes across 1 end of the cardboard cottage. **Ask the grown-up** to use the knife to cut another 10 sugar cubes in half. Brick up the wall in the same way you did the front, using the half cubes on the end of every other row.

For the 12th row, use only 8 cubes and begin bricking at the middle of the last row. Continue to add rows, using 1 less sugar cube for each row until you end up with only 1 cube. This will create a gabled rooftop. Brick the wall for the other end of the cottage in the same way.

4. To keep the walls from leaning as they dry, support them with 4 heavy books covered in plastic wrap. Place 1 book against the bricks on each side. Let it sit undisturbed overnight.

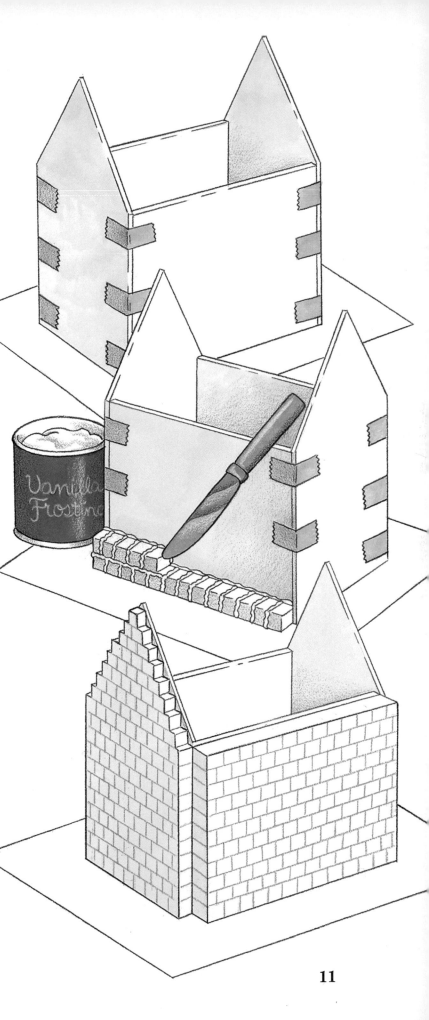

11

Making the Chimney

1. Remove the books from the sides of the cottage.

2. Stand 1 peanut butter wafer bar on 1 end. With the bottom edges of the bar and cottage lined up, place 1 long side of the bar along the center of the side of the cottage. Use the vanilla frosting to glue it in place. Glue another bar alongside of the first one. Then glue 2 more whole bars above these as shown.

3. Cut 1 peanut butter bar in half widthwise. Using the frosting, glue 1 piece to each side of the bottom of the 2 whole bars as shown.

4. Spread frosting generously on all sides of the chimney.

Making the Roof

1. Spoon a thick layer of vanilla frosting along the top edges of all 4 sides of the cottage. To form the peak in the roof, spread frosting on both short ends of 2 graham crackers. Press the 2 ends together. Carefully place the crackers on top of the cottage as shown. Gently press the roof section in place. Make 2 more sections and add them to the cottage in the same way. (Don't worry about the gaps or open areas. They will be covered with frosting later.) Let the cottage stand undisturbed overnight.

2. Spread a layer of frosting over the roof, covering the graham crackers and filling in all the open areas.

3. For the shingles, use the frosting to glue the butter cookies across the roof as shown.

4. Gently push the roll candies into the frosting across the top of the roof.

5. Place ½ cup of the frosting in a small bowl. Add 1 teaspoon of water at a time, stirring the mixture until it is the consistency of white glue. Dribble the mixture over the roof of the cottage to create the look of snow. Sprinkle nonpariels over the mixture. Let the cottage stand undisturbed overnight.

Decorating the Cottage

1. Using the frosting, glue the peppermint sticks to each corner of the cottage. Glue a jujube bear at the top of each peppermint stick. Seal any open corners with frosting.

2. From the fruit rolls, cut 1 (3″ x 2″) piece for the door, 2 (1½″) squares for windows, and 1 (2″-wide) semicircle for a window above the door. Use frosting to glue the door and windows to the front of the cottage.

3. Cut 2 sticks of chewing gum in half lengthwise. With the frosting, glue 1 piece of the gum to each side of the door. Cut 1 of the pieces to fit across the top of the door and glue it in place. Glue the candy button to the door for the door knob.

4. Cut 9 sticks of gum into thin strips and glue them to the windows.

5. Using the provided writing tip, pipe the decorating frosting above the door for a garland. Press nonpariels into the frosting. Pipe a wreath on the door and on the chimney. Press cinnamon candies in the frosting. For the window boxes, pipe frosting across the base of each window. Press the flower sprinkles into the frosting.

Evergreen Trees

You will need (for 4 trees):
A grown-up
Serrated knife
4 pointed ice cream cones
2 (4½-ounce) cans of green decorating
  frosting, with tips
Tiny-size flavor-coated gum
½ cup of ready-to-spread vanilla frosting
Teaspoon
Metal seive
¼ cup of powdered sugar

1. To make the trees different heights,
ask the grown-up to use the knife to
saw off part of the wide end of the cones.

2. Use the star tip provided with the
green frosting and pipe frosting all over
the cones.

3. To decorate the trees, press the gum
into the frosting. Let stand overnight.

4. Place about ½ cup of vanilla frosting
in a small bowl. Add 1 teaspoon of water
at a time, stirring the mixture until it's
the consistency of white glue. Dribble the
mixture over the top of the trees to create
the look of snow.

5. Place a small amount of powdered
sugar in the sieve and shake the sugar
over the trees.

Snowman

You will need:
⅓ cup ready-to-spread vanilla frosting
½ cup of powdered sugar
Additional ready-to-spread frosting
Scissors
1 (½-ounce) chewy fruit roll
1 tiny-size piece of flavor-coated gum
1 circular roll candy

1. Combine the ⅓ cup of frosting and the
powdered sugar, stirring until they are
well blended. Knead the mixture until it's
smooth and pliable like dough.

2. Shape the mixture into 3 different-
size balls for a snowman. Use the additional frosting to glue the balls together.

3. For the scarf, cut a 3″ x ¼″ strip from
the fruit roll. Use frosting to glue the
scarf to the snowman.

4. For the hat, use frosting to glue the
gum to the roll candy. Glue the hat to the
snowman with the frosting. Then let the
snowman stand undisturbed overnight.

14

Cottage End

Cut 2 from cardboard.

Mrs. Santa's Aprons

Before Mrs. Santa's helpers scoop the first cup of sugar or sift an ounce of flour, they first slip on her workshop aprons. Trace the stencil pattern and pull out the paint and a brush to make an apron just like Mrs. Santa's.

You will need (for each apron):
A grown-up
Craft knife
Tracing paper and pencil
1 sheet of stencil plastic
Masking tape
1 purchased red canvas apron
Newspaper
Paper plate
Green fabric paint
1″ foam paintbrush
Assortment of buttons and pom-poms
Tacky glue

1. Trace and cut out the stencil pattern. Trace the shaded areas of the pattern onto the plastic. **Ask the grown-up** to cut out the design with the craft knife.

2. Center the stencil on the right side of the apron bib, with the top of the house about 1″ from the top of the apron. Tape the stencil in place.

3. Cover your work surface with newspaper. Pour a little paint onto the paper plate and then paint the design green. Do not remove the stencil yet. Let the paint dry. If the design isn't dark enough, apply a second coat of paint. Remove the stencil when the paint is dry.

4. Glue on the buttons and pom-poms.

18

Cut out.

Cut out.

Cut out.

Cut out.

Peppermint Skates

At the North Pole, when it's too cold to play outside, the elves head to the Peppermint Raceway. They slip on their skates that Mrs. Santa made and the races begin. You'll find that these skates are too little for people to wear, but not too little to eat—they're a delicious peppermint treat.

You will need (for 6 pairs):
1 (16-ounce) can of ready-to-spread frosting
Plastic zip-top bag
Scissors
Waxed paper
12 peanut-shaped peanut butter sandwich cookies
48 round peppermint candies
12 candy-coated chocolate pieces
18 sticks of red cinnamon-flavored chewing gum
12 candy buttons

1. Spoon about ½ cup of frosting into the plastic bag. Push out all the air and then seal the bag. Snip 1 bottom corner of the bag with scissors to make a decorating bag. Set the bag aside.

2. Cover your work surface with waxed paper. Place the cookies on the paper.

3. For the wheels, pipe icing on the lower half of 1 peppermint candy. Press the candy to the side of the cookie as shown. The frosting will act as glue and hold the candy and cookie together. Glue 3 more peppermint wheels to the cookie in the same way.

4. Using the frosting, glue 1 candy-coated chocolate piece on 1 end of the cookie for a break stopper. Leave the skate upside down and undisturbed overnight.

5. For the heel strap and foot strap, cut 1 stick of chewing gum in half lengthwise. Turn the skate over so that it is standing on its wheels. Bend 1 piece of the gum so that it forms a semicircle. Coat the ends of this piece with frosting and glue it to 1 end of the skate between the 2 peppermint wheels. Hold the gum in place for a few seconds until it sticks. Glue the other piece of gum to the other end of the skate in the same way.

6. To make the ankle strap, cut another stick of gum in half lengthwise. Set 1 piece aside to use for another skate. Bend the other piece so that it forms a semicircle and coat the ends with frosting. Glue the ankle strap to the heel strap as shown. With frosting, glue 1 candy button on 1 side of the ankle strap. Let the skate stand undisturbed overnight.

7. Make the other skates in the same way.

Comet's Kaleidoscope

Most kaleidoscopes contain mirrors and loose bits of glass that create a variety of colorful patterns. But not at the North Pole! Comet, one of Santa's reindeer, uses reflective paper and candy to make kaleidoscopes. The only problem with his kaleidoscope is that someone keeps eating the candy.

You will need:
A grown-up
2½"-diameter art tube
  or mailing tube
Scissors
Wrapping paper
Glue
Measuring tape
7½" x 13" piece of
  posterboard
7½" x 13" piece of self-
  adhesive reflective paper
1 set of 2½"-diameter
  acrylic screw-together
  hook and tackle holders
Assorted small candies

1. Remove the end caps from the art tube. **Ask the grown-up** to cut out a ½" circle in the center of 1 cap. Set the other cap aside.

2. Cover the outside of the tube with wrapping paper and glue the edges in place.

3. To make the reflective triangular piece for the inside of the tube, cover 1 side of the posterboard with the reflective paper. (If you are using a different size tube, measure the tube's diameter and length. Cut the posterboard and reflective paper the same length as the tube but 3 times the diameter.)

4. Making sure the reflective paper is on the inside, fold and crease the covered posterboard every 2″ to form a long triangular shape that will fit inside the tube. Tape the long sides of the posterboard together. Then slip the triangle inside the tube.

5. Separate the acrylic containers from one another by unscrewing them. Fill 2 containers with candy and screw them back together. Screw an empty container to the top container. Slip the end of this container into 1 end of the tube.

6. Place the end cap with the hole in the middle on the other end of the tube. Hold the tube up to the light. Look through the small circle in the cap and watch the candy reflections change as you turn the tube.

Prancer's Peanut Butter Dough

Prancer loves to help Mrs. Santa in the kitchen. One day while baking peanut butter cookies, Prancer was distracted and forgot to add some of the ingredients. He discovered his dough wasn't good for cookies, but it was great for making other things—like dinosaurs or castles.

You will need (for 8 cups):
5 cups of instant nonfat dry milk powder
4 cups of smooth peanut butter
3 cups of honey
Large mixing bowl
Large wooden spoon
4 zip-top bags

1. Combine all the ingredients in the bowl. Stir until everything is well blended. The mixture will be very stiff.

2. Turn the dough out onto a clean work surface and knead it until it becomes soft and pliable.

3. Divide the dough into 4 portions. Put each portion in a separate bag. You can store the bags in the refrigerator up to 2 weeks.

Level 1

Reindeer Games

Tic-tac-toe is a fun game—but when reindeer at the North Pole play, the winner gets to eat all the game pieces, making it a delicious game! Mrs. Santa makes these tic-tac-toe sets to give to her reindeer friends. Each set has one game board and two different kinds of crackers for markers.

You will need:
1 (½-ounce) chewy fruit roll
Ruler
Kitchen shears
1 small tube of cake-decorating writing
    gel
Plastic wrap
1 (6-ounce) package of bite-size
    fish-shaped crackers
1 (10-ounce) box of bite-size round snack
    crackers

1. Unroll the fruit roll and press it flat. Remove the cellophane and throw it away. Using the kitchen shears, cut the roll into a 4½″ x 3½″ rectangle.

2. Using even pressure, lightly squeeze the gel and draw a tic-tac-toe grid on the fruit roll as shown.

3. Lightly cover the rectangle with plastic wrap and let it stand overnight at room temperature.

4. Use the fish-shaped crackers as 1 set of game pieces and the round crackers as the other set.

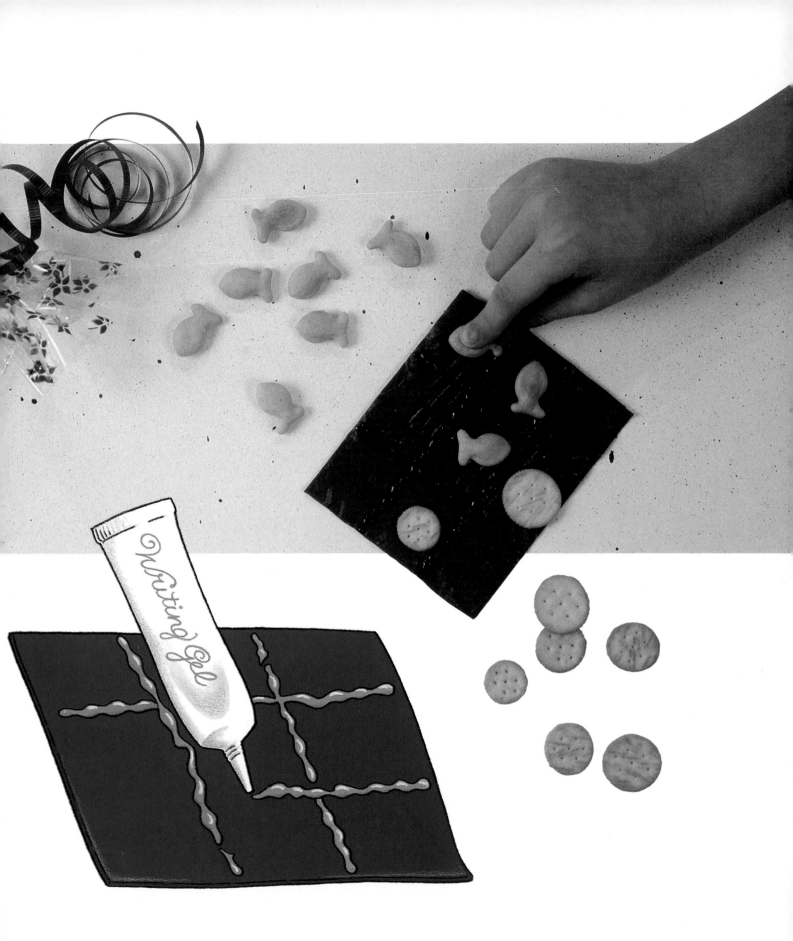

Bubblegum Baubles

String gum balls on dental floss to make colorful and tasty necklaces and bracelets for all your friends. It's as easy as blowing bubbles!

You will need (for 1 necklace and 1 bracelet):

A grown-up
Ice pick
20 to 26 candy-coated gum balls
42″ of dental floss
Large-eyed needle

1. **Ask the grown-up** to pierce a hole all the way through each gum ball with the ice pick.

2. For the necklace, cut a 30″ piece from the dental floss. Tie a knot in 1 end of the floss. Tie a double knot about 7″ from the first knot.

3. Thread the needle with the floss. String 15 to 18 balls onto the floss for the necklace. Remove the needle and tie a double knot in the floss next to the last ball. Tie a second knot in the end of the floss.

4. Use the remaining floss for the bracelet. Tie a knot in 1 end and a double knot about 5″ from the first knot. String 5 to 8 balls onto the floss. Complete the bracelet in the same way as the necklace.

North Pole Paint Set

When the elves at the North Pole pull out their paints and brushes, they know they are in for a treat—a sweet treat! Instead of painting with water colors, they use candy colors developed from an old elfin recipe. If you know a painter with a sweet tooth, here's the perfect gift.

You will need (for 3 sets):
3 cups of powdered sugar
2 tablespoons of water
Medium-size mixing bowl
Paste food coloring: blue, red, green, yellow
Craft stick
6 (1.25-ounce) creamy white candy bars with almonds
12 small plastic containers with lids
3 small paintbrushes

1. Combine the sugar and water in the bowl. Stir the mixture until it is smooth and creamy.

2. Divide the mixture evenly among 4 small bowls. With the craft stick, add food coloring, a little bit at a time, to each bowl until you achieve the color you want. Divide each color into 3 small plastic containers. Cover each one tightly.

3. Place 2 candy bars, 1 container of each color of paint, and 1 paintbrush in a bag or box for wrapping. Wrap the other 2 sets in the same way.

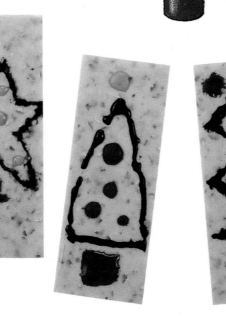

Stardust Wands

This sweet-and-sour powdered treat
will be fun to eat straight from Mrs.
Santa's Stardust Wands. If you follow
her secret recipe, you'll have plenty
of ingredients to make four wands
for friends and enough stardust
leftover for yourself.

You will need (for 4 wands):

1 (1-pound) box of instant dissolving
   sugar
1 (4-ounce) container of red sugar crystals
½ (7.5-ounce) container of orange-flavored
   breakfast beverage mix
1 (.13-ounce) package of cherry-flavored
   unsweetened soft drink mix
Large mixing bowl
Large wooden spoon
Zip-top plastic bag
Tracing paper
Pencil
Scissors
Posterboard
Dot stickers in assorted sizes
4 (9″ x 36″) pieces of net
4 pipe cleaners
Tacky glue
4 (12″) pieces of clear plastic tubing
½″-wide red plastic tape
8 corks to fit the ends of the tubes
Funnel

1. To make about 3 cups of stardust, combine the first 4 ingredients in the bowl. Stir them together until everything is well blended. Store the mixture in the zip-top bag until you're ready to fill the tubes.

2. Trace the star pattern and cut it out. From the posterboard, cut 1 star for each wand. Decorate each star with stickers.

3. Gather together 1 piece of net. Wrap a pipe cleaner around the middle of the net to make a bow. Glue a star to the net, covering the pipe cleaner. Do the same thing to make 3 more bows.

4. Starting at 1 end, wrap 1 tube with the red tape to resemble a candy cane. Repeat for the other 3 tubes.

5. Push a cork in 1 end of the tube so it fits very tightly. Place the funnel in the opposite end. While you hold the funnel, have a friend pour the stardust into the funnel to fill the tube. When it's full, push a cork in the open end. Place a dot sticker on the end of each cork. Fill the other 3 tubes in the same way.

6. To add the bow, twist the ends of the pipe cleaner around 1 end of the tube. Finish decorating the other tubes the same way.

Star

Santa's Dominoes

Santa loves dominoes and chocolate, so Mrs. Santa combined two of his favorite things—and made Chocolate Dominoes.

To play this game, you simply match the number of candy dots. Be careful, though! If the players are hungry the number of dots might change.

You will need (for 1 set of 28):
4 (13-ounce) packages of commercial fudge brownies
14 dozen small candy pieces
1 small tube of cake-decorating writing gel
Butter knife
Plastic wrap

1. Unwrap the brownies and place them upside down on a clean work surface. Using the butter knife, lightly score a line widthwise across the center of each brownie to form 2 sections.

2. To form domino designs, press 1 to 6 candy pieces into the sections as shown.

3. Using even pressure, squeeze the gel across the scored line on each brownie. Lightly cover the dominoes with plastic wrap and let them stand overnight at room temperature.

Children's Workshop
Happy Holiday Crafts

Candy Garland

Drape your doorway with a gigantic "candy" garland. Made from Styrofoam bowls and cellophane, this garland should withstand even a winter shower.

You will need:

16 (12-ounce) Styrofoam bowls
20″-wide colored cellophane: 5 feet each of
   blue, red, and green; 10 feet yellow
32 twist ties
8 feet of rope
16 gold pipe cleaners

1. Cut the blue, red, and green cellophane into 4 (20″ x 15″) pieces each. Cut the yellow cellophane into 8 (20″ x 15″) pieces. Cut the pipe cleaners in half.

2. Stack 2 pieces of yellow cellophane on a flat surface. Place the base of 1 bowl in the center and wrap both pieces of cellophane over the bowl. Twist each end of the cellophane tightly and secure with a twist tie. Repeat with the rest of the yellow cellophane and 3 more bowls.

3. Use just 1 piece of cellophane at a time to wrap each of the remaining bowls. Twist each end tightly and secure with a twist tie.

4. Lay the rope down on a flat surface. Beginning about 12″ from 1 end of the rope, start attaching the candy. Take 2 matching color bowls and place the flat rim sides together with the rope sandwiched in between them. To hold the bowls together and to attach them to the rope, wrap a pipe cleaner piece around the ends over the twist ties. Attach all the remaining bowls to the rope in the same way.

Christmas Tree Skirt

Wrap some felt rectangles with ribbons and glue them to this easy-to-make green felt tree skirt. That way you'll always be sure to find packages under your Christmas tree even if Santa hasn't made his visit yet.

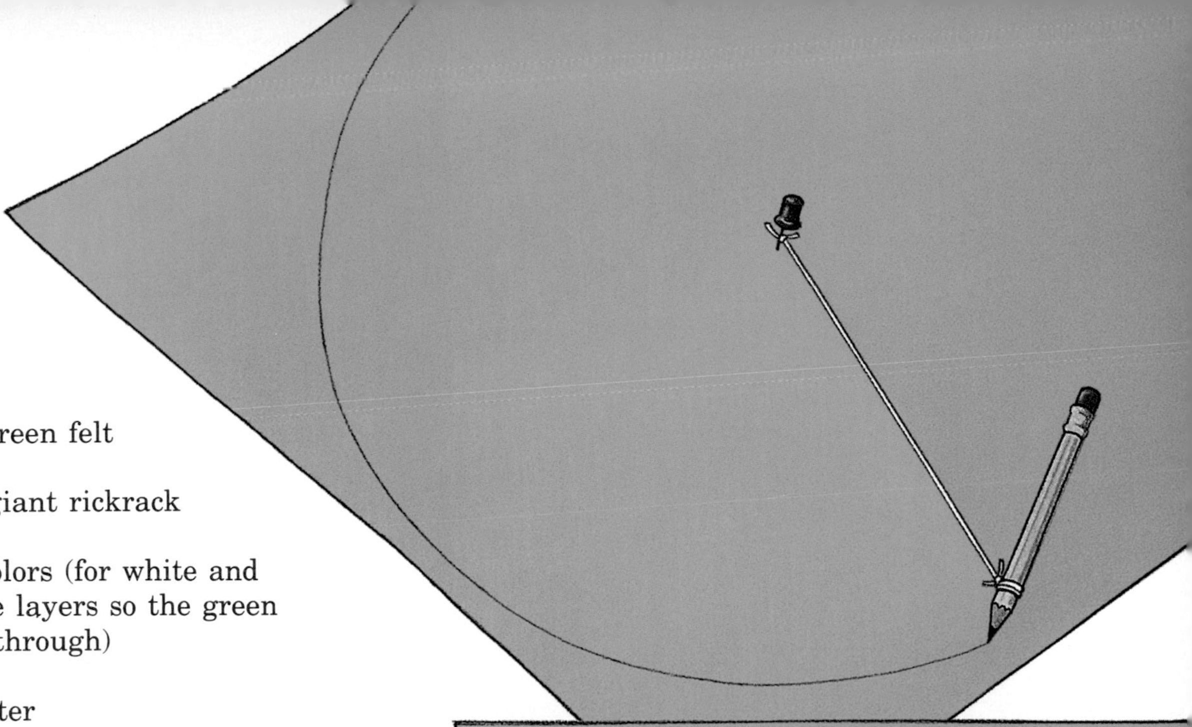

You will need:

Pencil or marker
Pushpin
36″ of string
2 yards (72″-wide) green felt
Scissors
7½ yards of white giant rickrack
Fabric glue
Felt rectangles: 8 colors (for white and
   yellow, use double layers so the green
   felt doesn't show through)
Variety of ribbons
Liquid ravel preventer
Twist ties
Ruler

1. To make a compass, tie the pencil to 1
end of the string and the pushpin to the
other end. Stick the pushpin in the center
of the felt. With the string and pencil,
draw a large circle. Cut the string to 5″
and make a smaller circle in the center of
the large circle. Cut out the large circle.
Cut straight up from the edge of the large
circle to the small circle and then cut out
the small circle to make an opening for
the tree trunk.

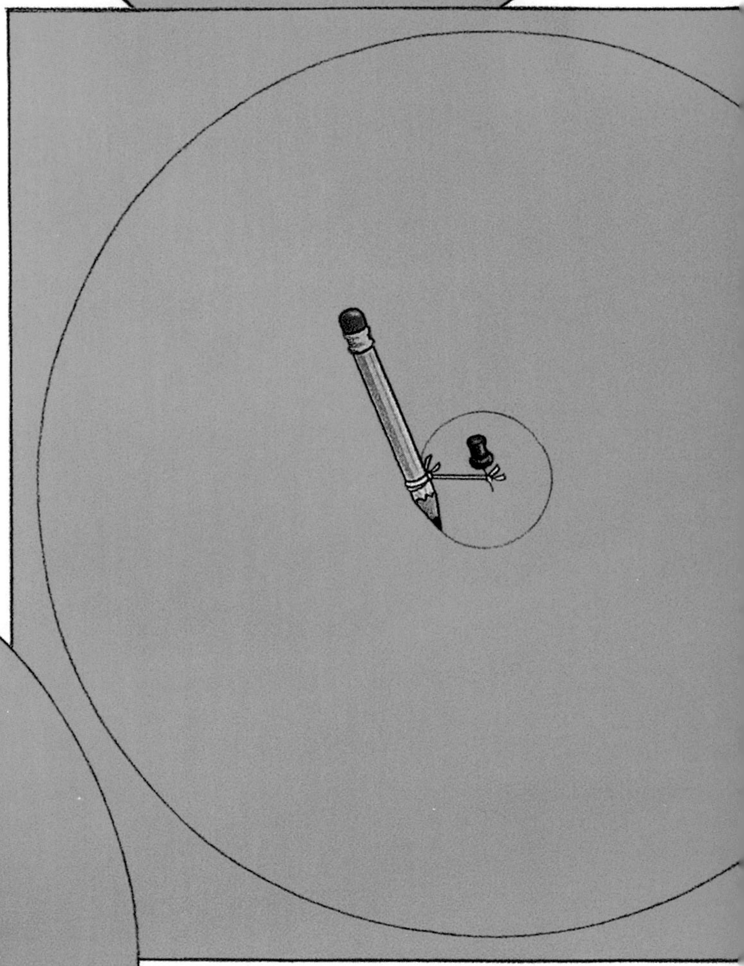

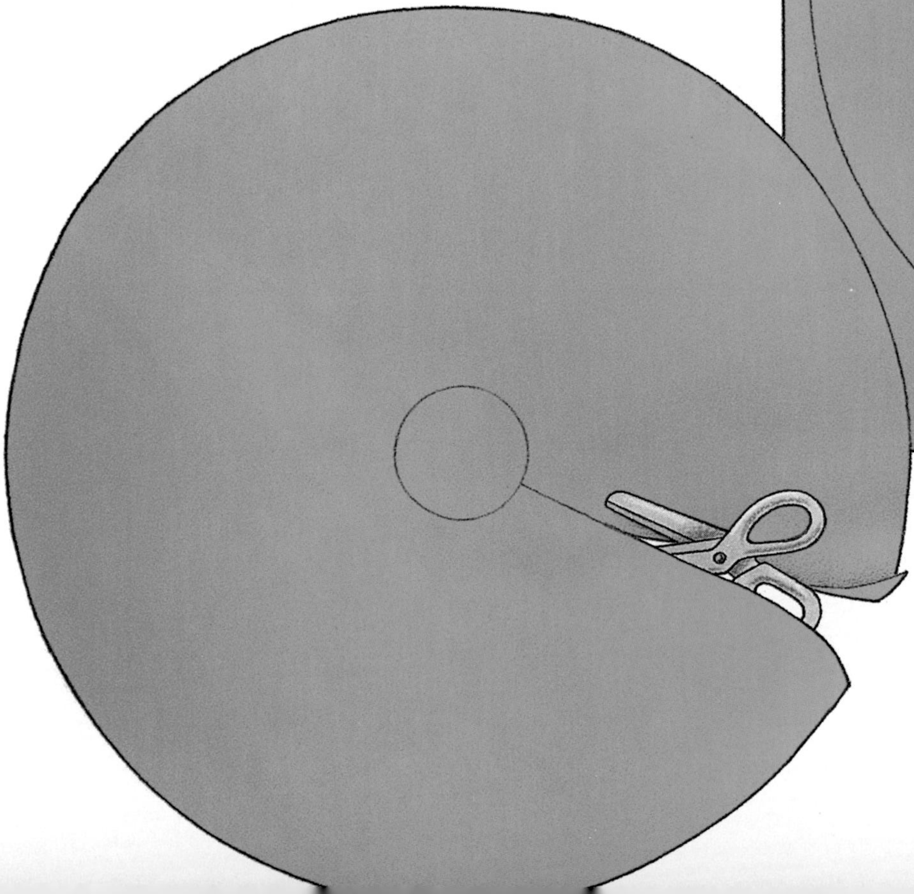

2. With fabric glue, glue the rickrack to the inner and outer edges of the circle. Apply liquid ravel preventer to the ends of the rickrack to keep the ends from fraying.

3. To make the packages, choose ribbons to coordinate with each felt rectangle. Measure across the width, or down the length, or even diagonally across a corner of the felt. Cut the ribbon that length. Apply liquid ravel preventer to the ribbon ends so they won't fray. Let the ends dry. Then glue the ribbon to the felt. With the twist ties and the same ribbon or another coordinating ribbon, make a bow to add to the top of the package. Glue the bow in place. Decorate all the felt rectangles with ribbons.

4. Place the packages around the skirt, about 7½″ from the outer edge. Once you have all the packages arranged the way you want, glue them in place. Let the glue dry.

Oodles of Noodles

Macaroni comes in lots of shapes and sizes. The shapes used for these ornaments are wagon wheels and small and large bow ties. But when the macaroni is glued and painted, it'll be hard to tell they were once just oodles of noodles.

Trees

You will need:
A grown-up
Waxed paper
Founder's Adhesive glue
11 wagon wheel macaronis
Green spray paint
10 small red decorative balls
6″ of gold thread

1. Cover your work surface with waxed paper. To form the tree, glue the wagon wheels together in rows as follows. Row 1 has only 1 wheel. Glue 2 wheels together for Row 2. Glue 3 wheels together for Row 3. Glue 4 wheels together for Row 4. Then glue the 4 rows together as shown. For the tree trunk, glue 1 wheel at the center of the bottom row. Let the glue dry.

2. Ask the grown-up to help you spray-paint both sides of the tree. Be sure to do this outside or in a well-ventilated room. Let the paint dry.

3. Glue the red balls in the center of each wheel on Rows 1–4.

4. To make a hanger, slip the gold thread through the top opening in the top wheel and knot the ends of the thread.

Bow Tie Wreaths

You will need:
A grown-up
Waxed paper
Founder's Adhesive glue
7 bow tie macaroni
4 small egg bow macaroni
Spray paint: green, red
Gold glitter paint
6″ of gold thread

1. Cover your work surface with waxed paper. Glue 6 bow tie macaronis together in a circle, slightly overlapping their edges. Let them dry.

2. Ask the grown-up to help you spray-paint the wreath green. Let it dry. For the bows, spray-paint the remaining bow tie and 4 small egg bow macaronis red. Let them dry.

3. Glue the large red bow to the top of the wreath, overlapping 2 green macaronis as shown.

4. Glue the small red bows to the center of the remaining green bows.

5. Dot the center of the red bows with glitter paint.

6. For a hanger, fold the gold thread in half and glue the ends to the top back of the wreath.

Glitter Ornaments

Glue plus glitter
equals a golden holiday.
When light hits the tiny particles of
gold on these ornaments, your tree
will sparkle from every branch.

Glitter Sticks

You will need (for 1 ornament):
Waxed paper
8" of gold thread
Glue
Wooden craft stick
Paintbrush
Gold glitter

1. Cover your work surface with waxed paper.

2. To make the hanger, fold the thread in half and glue the ends to the craft stick. Let the glue dry.

3. Using the paintbrush, spread 1 side of the craft stick with glue. Sprinkle glitter over the glue. Let the glue dry. Then spread glue and sprinkle glitter on the other side of the stick.

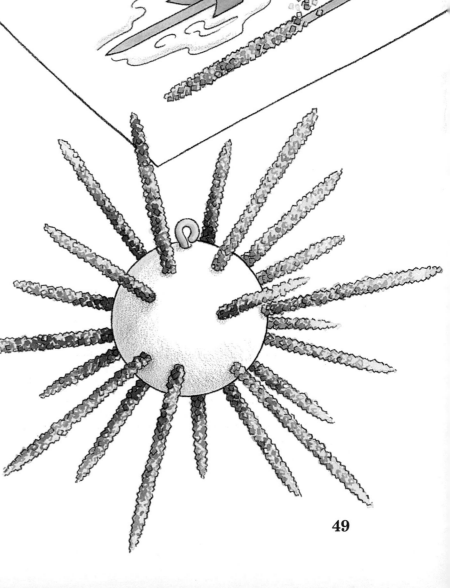

Star Brights

You will need (for 1 ornament):
Waxed paper
Brass screw eye
1 (1½"-diameter) Styrofoam ball
Glue
50 wooden toothpicks
Gold glitter
8" of gold thread

1. Cover your work surface with waxed paper.

2. Push the screw eye into the center top of the ball.

3. Squeeze some glue on the waxed paper. Roll each toothpick in the glue. Place the toothpicks on the waxed paper and sprinkle them with glitter. Turn the toothpicks over and sprinkle them again. Let them dry.

4. Push each toothpick into the ball, using the diagram as a guide.

5. To make the hanger, slip the gold thread through the screw eye and knot the ends together.

49

Sticky-Star Balls

You will need (for 1 ornament):
Waxed paper
Brass screw eye
1 (2½" to 4"-diameter) Styrofoam ball
Toothpick
Glue
Gold glitter
Gold self-adhesive stars
12" (½"-wide) gold ribbon
8" of gold thread

1. Cover your work surface with waxed paper.

2. Push the screw eye into the center top of the ball.

3. Using the toothpick, spread some glue onto the ball. Sprinkle the ball with glitter and let it dry.

4. Decorate the ball as desired with the star stickers. (If the stars don't stick to the ball, glue them in place.)

5. Thread half of the ribbon through the screw eye and tie it in a bow.

6. To make the hanger, slip the gold thread through the screw eye and knot the ends together.

Holiday Doorkeepers

Ready to welcome holidays and friends are a playful trio of Santa, an angel, and a snowman. Although they are made from extra-heavy paper plates, they still prefer to greet visitors indoors— winter winds are not their friends.

You will need (for each doorkeeper):

Waxed paper
2 (10½″) heavy-duty
 paper plates
Paintbrushes
White glue
Scissors
Stapler
Hole punch
20″ of thin cording
White glitter

For the angel:

Acrylic paints: yellow, pink
12″ piece of gold tinsel garland
18″ piece of ribbon
2 (7/16″) blue buttons
1 (5/8″) pearl button
1 (½″) pink heart button
Gold glitter

For Santa:

Acrylic paints: red, pink, white
1 (2″) white pom-pom
2 (7/8″) black buttons
1 (1″) red glitter pom-pom
2 jingle bells

For the snowman:

Acrylic paints: turquoise, white, purple,
 green
1 (2″) white pom-pom
2 (1⅛″) black buttons
5 (½″) red buttons
3 (1″) orange pom-poms
2 jingle bells

Before you begin: Cover your work surface with waxed paper. When shaking off excess glitter, catch it on the waxed paper and put it back into the container.

Angel Doorkeeper

1. For the angel's neck, lightly mark off a 3″ section on the rim of 1 plate with a pencil. Cut away a 2″ piece on each side of the 3″ section.

2. Referring to the diagram, paint the angel's hair yellow and let it dry. Paint the face pink and let it dry.

3. Randomly spread a thin coat of glue on the angel's hair. Also spread glue on the cheeks. Sprinkle white glitter over these areas. Let the glue dry. Gently shake off the extra glitter.

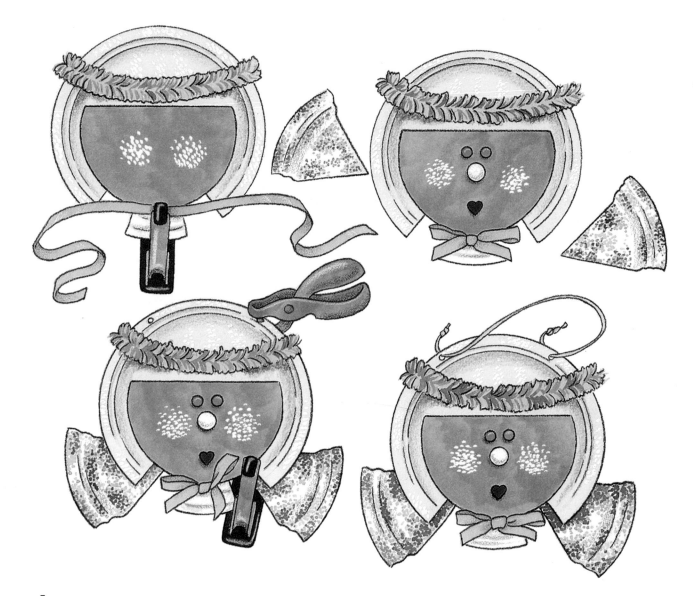

4. For the halo, staple the ends of the garland to the rim of the plate. Staple the center of the ribbon to the collar and tie the ends to make a bow.

5. Glue on the button eyes, nose, and mouth. Let the glue dry.

6. From the other plate, cut 2 pie-shape sections for wings. Using a paintbrush, coat the wings with a thin layer of glue. Sprinkle them with gold glitter. Let the glue dry. Shake off the extra glitter. Staple the wings to the angel and cover the

staples with matching paint. Let them dry.

7. At the top of the plate, punch 2 holes about 6″ apart. For the hanger, tie several big knots at 1 end of the cording. From the back of the plate, thread the unknotted end of the cording through 1 of the holes. From the front of the plate, push the unknotted end of the cording through the other hole and knot the end.

Santa Doorkeeper

1. Paint the top third of 1 plate red for Santa's hat. Leave a 1¾″ strip unpainted for the hat trim. Paint the rest of the plate pink for the face. Let the paint dry.

2. Glue the white pom-pom on the hat trim and the button eyes on the face. Let the glue dry.

3. For Santa's beard, cut a 4½″-deep piece from the other plate. Staple it in place over the face. Paint the staples white. Glue on the red pom-pom nose and let it dry.

4. For the hanger, follow Step 7 in the directions for the angel but string the bells on the cording after the cording is thread through the first hole. Slide a bell down over each of the holes.

5. Using a paintbrush, spread a thin coat of glue on the cheeks and randomly on Santa's hat. Spread glue all over the hat trim and beard. Sprinkle glitter over these areas. Let the glue dry. Shake off the extra glitter.

54

Snowman Doorkeeper

1. For the snowman's hat, paint the top half of 1 plate turquoise. Let it dry. Paint white polka dots on the hat and let them dry.

2. Using a paintbrush, spread a thin coat of glue on the polka dots and on the unpainted half of the plate (face). Sprinkle glitter over these areas and let it dry. Gently shake off the extra glitter.

3. Referring to the photo, glue on the white pom-pom, the button eyes, the button mouth, and 1 orange pom-pom nose. Let them dry. Glue another orange pom-pom on top of the first one. When it is dry, glue the third orange pom-pom to the second one and let it dry.

4. To make the scarf, cut a 10″ piece from the rim of the other plate. Cut the ends of the scarf with scissors to make fringe. Paint the scarf purple and let it dry. Then paint green stripes and polka dots. Let the paint dry. Staple the scarf to the snowman and paint over the staples with matching paint.

5. For the hanger, follow Step 7 in the directions for the angel but string the bells on the cording. Slide a bell down over each of the holes.

Ribbon Candy

They may look good enough to eat, but these ribbon candies are strictly treats for the tree. Collect scraps of striped ribbon or find ribbons in Christmas colors to make a wide assortment of "flavors."

You will need:
A grown-up
Waxed paper
Liquid fabric stiffener
Paintbrush
Craft ribbons: 12″ (⅝″–¾″-wide) lengths,
   24″ (1½″-wide) lengths
Rustproof, fine straight pins
Flat piece of Styrofoam
Pliers (optional)
Scissors
Sharp needle
Silver thread

1. Cover your work space with waxed paper.

2. Follow the directions on the fabric stiffener bottle and paint the stiffener on both sides of 1 piece of ribbon. Smooth the stiffener with the paintbrush for an even coat.

3. Stick a pin through the center of the ribbon into the Styrofoam. Form tight curls in the ribbon and hold them in place with more straight pins. Try to keep all the curls the same height, about ¾″ high for narrow ribbons and 1″ high for wide ribbons.

4. Leave the pins in place but lightly pull the ribbon away from the Styrofoam so the ribbon doesn't stick to the Styrofoam when the stiffener dries.

5. Let the ribbon dry thoroughly. **Ask the grown-up** to remove the pins from the ribbon, using the pliers if desired.

6. Cut 1 end of the ribbon curl into a point. To make a hanger, insert a 10″ length of thread through the tip of the point. Tie the ends of the thread together.

Nutty Reindeer Ornaments

Oh, nuts! That's about all it takes to make these nutty reindeer. This herd includes a peanut, a walnut, a Brazil nut, an almond, and a hazelnut. Create your own mixed herd, or choose your favorite nut and make a matching family.

You will need (for each):
A grown-up
Nut
Nutcracker
Pen
Tracing paper
Scissors
Green construction paper
Red felt
Tacky glue
10″ piece of red cord or ribbon
Toothpick
2 (7-mm) wiggle eyes
1 small red pom-pom

1. Ask the grown-up to help you crack the nut in half. Remove the meat from the shell. Choose the best-shaped shell half and set the other half aside.

2. Trace and cut out the antler pattern. Cut 1 pair of antlers from the green construction paper.

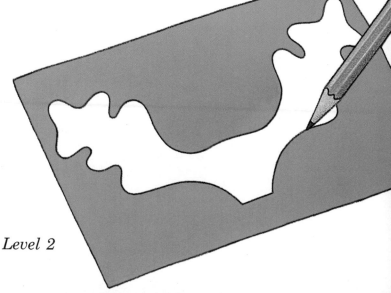

Level 2

3. For the ornament back, place the shell on the red felt and trace around it. Cut out the felt.

4. Glue the antlers to the back of the top or wider end of the nut. For the hanger, fold the cord in half and glue the 2 ends to the back of the antlers. Then glue the red felt to the back, covering the cord and the back of the antlers.

5. Squeeze a little glue onto the toothpick. Dab the glue on the back of the wiggle eyes. Glue the eyes in place. Glue on the red pom-pom nose. Let the ornament dry.

Antlers

Blue striped zebras and purple polka-dotted giraffes! These wonderful wild animals are ready for your holiday jubilee. Tie one to a package or use a bunch to brighten a wreath or tree.

You will need (for each animal):
Tracing paper
Pencil
Scissors
Fun Foam in assorted colors
Tacky glue
2 (3-mm) wiggle eyes
Needle
Monofilament thread

1. Trace and cut out the desired animal patterns.

2. Lay the pattern on the foam and trace around it.

3. Trace the other animal details on a contrasting color of foam. For the elephant, trace and cut out 2 ears. For the lion, trace and cut 2 manes and 1 face. Clip the edges of the manes to make the fringe.

Details for the other animals don't need patterns. Cut out stripes for the front and back of the zebra. Cut 6 tiny triangles for the alligator teeth. For the giraffe, cut out circles in various sizes and colors.

4. Glue 1 ear to each side of the elephant. Glue the lion's face to 1 mane. Glue the face/mane to 1 side of the body and the second mane to the other side of the body. Glue the stripes to both sides of the zebra. Glue 3 teeth to both sides of the alligator. Glue the circles to both sides of the giraffe.

5. Glue wiggle eyes on both sides of all the animals except the lion. (He's facing forward.)

6. For each hanger, cut a 10″ piece of monofilament thread. Thread the needle and run it through the top center of the animal. Tie the ends of the thread in a knot.

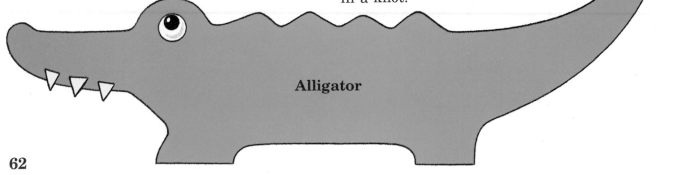

Alligator

Lion's mane
Cut 2.

Lion's face
Cut 1.

Lion

Elephant's
ear
Cut 2.

Elephant

Zebra

Giraffe

Wrap It Up!

It's a wrap! It may look like a decoration, but really there's a present hiding inside each vinyl package. Cut out these holiday shapes or use your imagination and see what shapes you can make.

You will need (for each wrap):
2 (11″ x 17″) pieces of clear
   lightweight vinyl
Permanent marker
Scissors
Hole punch
Glue
For the tree:
14 buttons in various shapes and colors
2 yards of red curling ribbon
Green tissue paper
For the stocking:
20″ of green jumbo rickrack
2 yards of green curling ribbon
Red tissue paper
For the star:
Gold glitter paint stick
Yellow star stickers
3 yards of yellow curling ribbon
Dark blue tissue paper

1. Decide what small gift you want to
wrap.

2. Stack the 2 vinyl rectangles together.
On the top one, use the marker to draw 1
of the simple shapes shown here, such as
a tree, stocking, or star, or draw your
own shape. Just make sure the shape is
large enough to hold the gift.

3. Cut out the 2 shapes at the same
time following the line. Hold the 2 layers
of vinyl together and punch holes about
1″ apart all around the outside edges of
the shape.

4. To decorate the front of the tree,
glue on buttons. To decorate the front
of the stocking, glue pieces of rickrack
on the toe, heel, and cuff. For the star,
decorate 1 side with glitter paint. Let it
dry. Place star stickers on the other side
of the star.

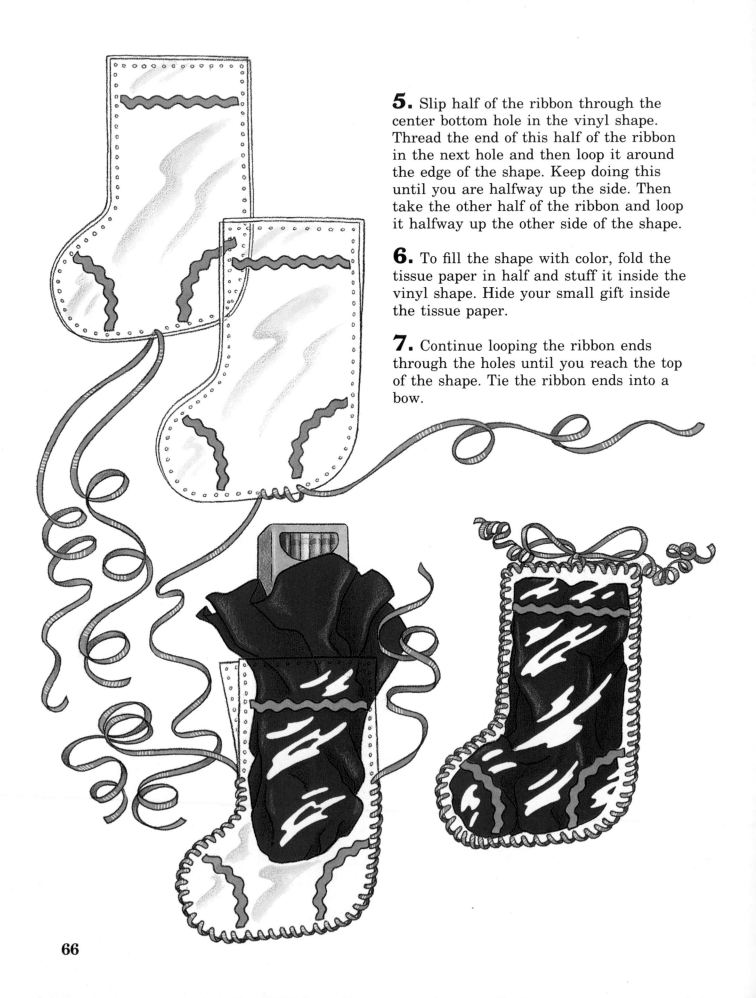

5. Slip half of the ribbon through the center bottom hole in the vinyl shape. Thread the end of this half of the ribbon in the next hole and then loop it around the edge of the shape. Keep doing this until you are halfway up the side. Then take the other half of the ribbon and loop it halfway up the other side of the shape.

6. To fill the shape with color, fold the tissue paper in half and stuff it inside the vinyl shape. Hide your small gift inside the tissue paper.

7. Continue looping the ribbon ends through the holes until you reach the top of the shape. Tie the ribbon ends into a bow.

Spoon Angel

3. Tear off a small clump of yellow shred and glue it to the back of the spoon over the ends of the hanger. Hold the shred in place until it sticks. Let the glue dry.

4. Bend the star garland to make a circle and twist the ends together. Slip the garland over the hanger loop and onto the top of the head.

5. Using the markers, draw a face.

For a holiday giggle, decorate your tree with this impish angel. A silly smile crowned with fanciful hair and a tilted halo transforms an ordinary plastic spoon into a whimsical Christmas ornament.

You will need:
10″ (3″-wide) foil craft ribbon
White plastic spoon
Scissors
12″ of fishing line
Cellophane tape
Yellow shred
Glue
5″ of multicolored star garland
Fine-point permanent markers: black, red

1. Tie the ribbon around the spoon handle. Trim and shape the ribbon ends.

2. For the hanger, fold the fishing line in half and knot the ends together. Tape the ends to the back of the spoon.

Greetings from Santa

This simple Santa will flip his beard for your friends—just to deliver your special Ho-Ho greetings. Make dozens to mail or to use as holiday gift tags.

You will need:
Tracing paper
Pencil
Scissors
Construction paper: red, white, black, pink
Fine-point black marker
Glue stick
White pom-pom

1. Trace and cut out the patterns.

2. From the red paper, cut out 1 triangle and 2 cheeks.

3. Fold the white paper in half. Place the beard pattern on the fold and cut 1. Also cut the hatband from the white paper.

4. From the black paper, cut the belt and hands. Cut the face from the pink paper. Use the marker to add the details.

5. Glue each piece in place on the large red triangle, beginning with the belt and hands. Glue the beard next, and then the face, the cheeks, and the hatband.

6. Glue the pom-pom to the tip of the hat.

7. Lift the beard and write your special greeting inside.

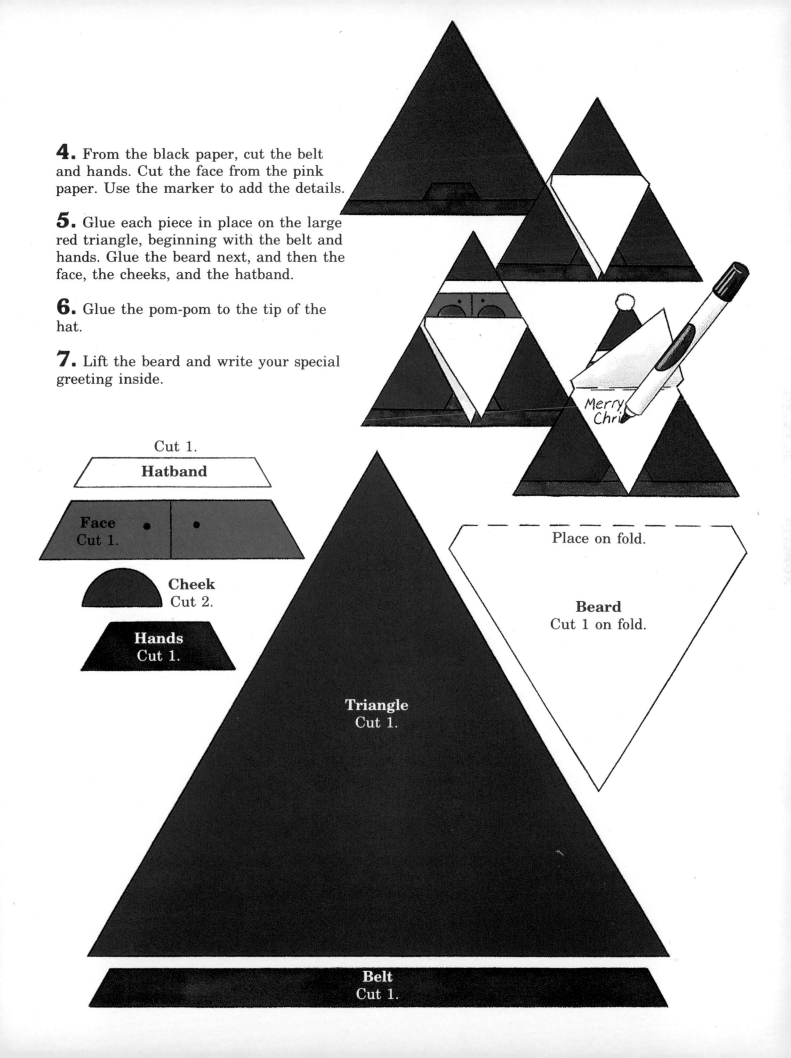

Cut 1.
Hatband

Face
Cut 1.

Cheek
Cut 2.

Hands
Cut 1.

Triangle
Cut 1.

Place on fold.

Beard
Cut 1 on fold.

Merry Chri

Belt
Cut 1.

Mailbox Cover

This mailbox cover will let Santa and all of your friends know that you're ready for Christmas deliveries. Slip it on at the start of the holiday season and let the festivities begin.

You will need:
Tape measure
½ yard of white weatherproof vinyl
Scissors
Pencil
Ruler
Acrylic paints: red, red-orange, yellow-orange, yellow, green, blue, light blue
Paintbrushes: ¼″ flat and #2 round
1 yard of magnetic strip tape
Tacky glue
3⅓ yards (1″-wide) red weatherproof ribbon

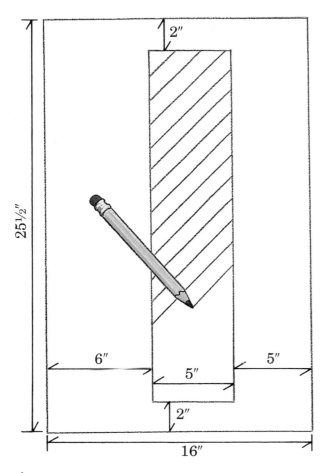

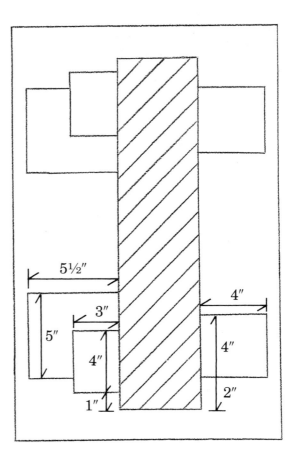

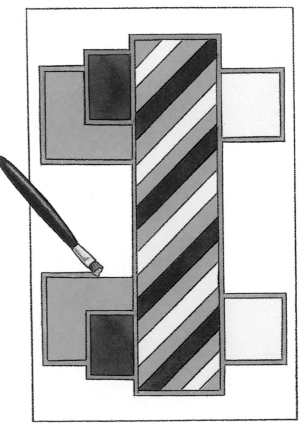

1. To fit a standard mailbox, cut a 16″ x 25½″ rectangle from the vinyl. If your mailbox is smaller or larger, measure and cut a rectangle to fit around it.

2. With the pencil and ruler, draw the tall center package all the way across the center of the vinyl rectangle, stopping 2″ from each end of the vinyl. Draw stripes on the package by slanting the ruler and drawing lines 1″ apart. Draw the other packages beside the tall package as shown.

3. Paint the packages as you like. Let each color dry before using another color. Outline the packages in light blue. Let the paint dry.

4. Add stars, holly, ribbons, and bows in contrasting colors. Let the paint dry. Outline the bows with light blue paint. Let them dry.

5. To hold the cover in place on the mailbox, cut 1 magnetic strip the width of the vinyl. On the wrong side of the vinyl, glue the strip in place on 1 end. Cut another magnetic strip and glue it to the opposite edge.

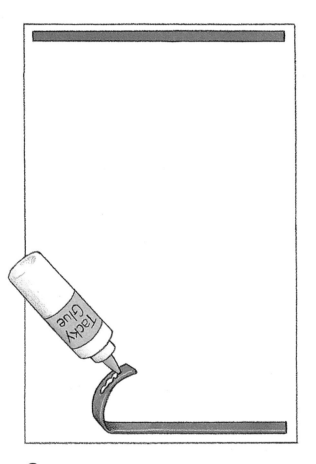

6. Slip the cover under the flag and around the mailbox. Stick the magnetic strips to the bottom of the mailbox.

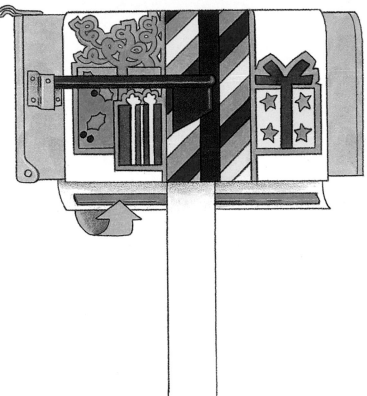

7. To make the ribbon bow, cut 12″ from 1 end of the ribbon and set it aside. Cut a 36″ piece and set it aside. To make a bow with the remaining ribbon, make 6 loops. Tie the loops in the center with the 12″ piece of ribbon. Tie the bow to the center of the 36″ piece.

Place the bow at the center of the top of the mailbox. Wrap the ribbon ends around the mailbox and tie them together underneath the mailbox. Tuck the ends out of sight.

There are bonnets and boaters that shield the sun. There are stocking caps and ski caps to keep in the warmth. But these hats have no practical purpose at all. They're just Crazy Hats! Decorate one for a friend to ensure year-round fun.

Red Hat

You will need:
1 straw hat
Founder's Adhesive glue
Craft stick
1 package of purple/pink metallic shred
2 yards of purple net
Pink glitter
Pipe cleaner

1. With the craft stick, spread a thin layer of glue on the brim of the hat. Then stick the shred to the glued area.

2. Randomly apply small spots of glue all over the net. Sprinkle the glitter over the glue. Let the glue dry; then shake off the extra glitter.

3. Gather up the net and wrap it around the hat to form a band. Tie the net together at the back of the hat with a pipe cleaner. Twist the ends of the pipe cleaner to form a bow. Let the remaining net drape behind the hat.

Pink Hat

You will need:
1 straw hat
Founder's Adhesive glue
Craft stick
2 packages of giant rickrack
Assorted plastic buttons, rings, and small
  toys

1. With the craft stick, glue the rickrack around the top edge of the brim, around the bottom edge of the brim, and around the band. Let it dry.

2. Glue the buttons, rings, and toys on the hat. Let them dry.

Yellow Hat

You will need:
1 straw hat
Founder's Adhesive glue
Craft stick
Plastic Hawaiian lei
Stapler
Rubber letter
Assorted balloons and feathers
2 hearts on springs
2 gold metallic pipe cleaners
8″ of crinkle ribbon
2 plastic grape clusters
2 brads

1. With the craft stick, apply glue around the edge of the brim. Stick the lei to the glued area. Let it dry.

2. Fold the hat brim up to touch the front of the hat. Staple the brim through the center of the hat to hold it in place.

3. Glue the letter to the center front of the brim over the staple. Glue 2 balloons on each side of the letter. Cut 1 pipe cleaner into 3 pieces. Glue the pieces together to make a star. Bend the ends to curl them. Glue the star over 1 pair of balloons. Do the same thing with the other pipe cleaner. Glue on the feathers and hearts to decorate the rest of the hat.

4. Cut the ribbon in half. To make the grape earrings, slip 1 end of 1 ribbon through the top of 1 grape cluster and tie the ribbon in a knot. Stick a brad through the other end of the ribbon and then into the brim from the underside of the hat. Fold back the ends of the brad on the top of the brim to secure it in place. Repeat for the other earring.

76

Surprise Balls

It's a present! No, it's an ornament. Actually, it's both! Simply find the plastic ornaments at your craft store—they come in all shapes and sizes. Then fill them with colorful surprises.

You will need:
Plastic ball ornaments that open
Golf tees, embroidery floss, jacks and ball, or other small gifts
Paper curling ribbon: red, green, gold

1. Decide who you want to give an ornament gift to and then choose a colorful surprise. The balls shown here are filled with tees for a golfer, embroidery floss for a stitcher, and jacks for a young friend. There are lots of other possibilities, so use your imagination and have fun!

2. Cut a 12″ piece each of red, green, and gold ribbon. Thread the ribbons through the opening at the top of the ornament and tie them in a knot. Carefully pull the edge of scissors across the ribbon to make it curl.

Level 1

77

Refrigerator Magnets

Stick 'em up! Your mom can use these colorful magnets to hang your artwork on the refrigerator gallery.

You will need:
Pencil
Tracing paper
Scissors
White foam trays (clean and dry)
Acrylic paints in assorted colors
Paintbrushes in assorted sizes
Squeeze tube of white acrylic paint
Roll of magnetic strip tape
White glue

1. Trace and cut out the patterns.

2. Trace the patterns on the tray and cut them out.

3. Paint the shapes. Let the paint dry. Add the details using a smaller paintbrush. Let the paint dry between colors.

4. Outline each shape with the squeeze paint. Let the paint dry completely.

5. Cut a piece of magnetic tape and glue it on the back of each shape.

Stocking

Candy Cane

Tree

Snowman

80

Angel

Gingerbread Man

Star

Present

Key Holder

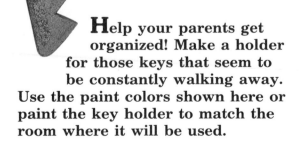

Help your parents get organized! Make a holder for those keys that seem to be constantly walking away. Use the paint colors shown here or paint the key holder to match the room where it will be used.

You will need:
A grown-up
6½" x 8½" piece of ½" plywood
Sandpaper
Old towel
Acrylic paints: white, black, turquoise,
  red, green
Paintbrushes
Tracing paper
Pencil
Scissors
Picture hanger and small nails
Small hammer
Ruler
4 (1") brass cup hooks

1. Sand the front, back, and edges of the board. Wipe it off with the towel.

2. Paint the entire board with several coats of white paint, letting the paint dry between coats.

3. Trace and cut out the pattern. On the front of the board, center the pattern for the car about ¾" from the top and lightly trace around it with the pencil. Then draw in the windows, door handle, and top of the wheels.

4. Paint the car turquoise and let it dry.

5. Paint the windows, door handle, and wheels black. Outline the car with black paint. Let the paint dry.

6. In the center of each wheel, paint a white circle. Then paint a small red circle with a smaller green circle inside it. Paint a green dot on the door handle. Let the paint dry between coats and colors.

7. Paint red polka dots around the car on the front of the board. Let them dry. Then paint the center of each polka dot turquoise. Paint red and turquoise stripes around all outside edges of the board. Let the paint dry.

8. Place the board right side down on the towel. Place the picture hanger at the top center of the back of the board. **Ask the grown-up** to nail it in place.

9. On the front of the board, place the end of the ruler at the left edge and about ¾″ from the bottom. Lightly mark across the board at 1¾″, 3½″, 5¼″, and 7″. Screw in a cup hook at each mark.

Bank on It

Recycle powdered drink and frosting containers to make individual banks for friends. They'll love investing—you can bank on it!

You will need (for 1 bank):
A grown-up
Plastic drink mix container with lid or ready-made icing container with lid
Paint markers
Craft knife

1. Remove the label from the container. Thoroughly wash and dry it.

2. With the paint markers, draw and color designs around the container. Add the name of the person who will receive the bank. Let the container dry.

3. Ask the grown-up to use the craft knife and cut an opening that measures 1⅛" x ¼" in the center of the lid.

4. Place the lid on the container.

Tags to Go

Tag that bag! For all those people you know who are on the go, why not make personalized tags for bags and keys. Then check out your sticker collection and you'll probably find the perfect stickers to decorate each and every one.

You will need (for 1 tag):
3″ x 5″ white card
Ruler
Pencil
Scissors
Pinking shears
Fine-point colored markers
Stickers: flowers, baby toys, sports
  emblems
Laminating sheet
Hole punch
Key chain or ring

1. Cut the card to the size you want. (A common size for a luggage tag is 2½″ x 3½″, but you could cut an oval or even a special shape like the tennis racket.) Pink the edges if you like.

2. Use the markers to write the name and address on the card. Decorate the card with stickers.

3. Cut 2 pieces from the laminating sheet, each ½″ larger than the card. Remove the backing from 1 laminating piece. Lay the piece on the table with the sticky side up. Place the right side of the card on the sticky side of the laminating piece. Remove the backing from the other laminating piece. Line up the edges and press the 2 laminating pieces together. Trim the edges of the laminating pieces so they are even and extend a little bit beyond the card.

4. Punch a hole with the hole punch close to 1 edge of the card. Attach the key chain or ring through the hole.

87

Decorated Dishtowels

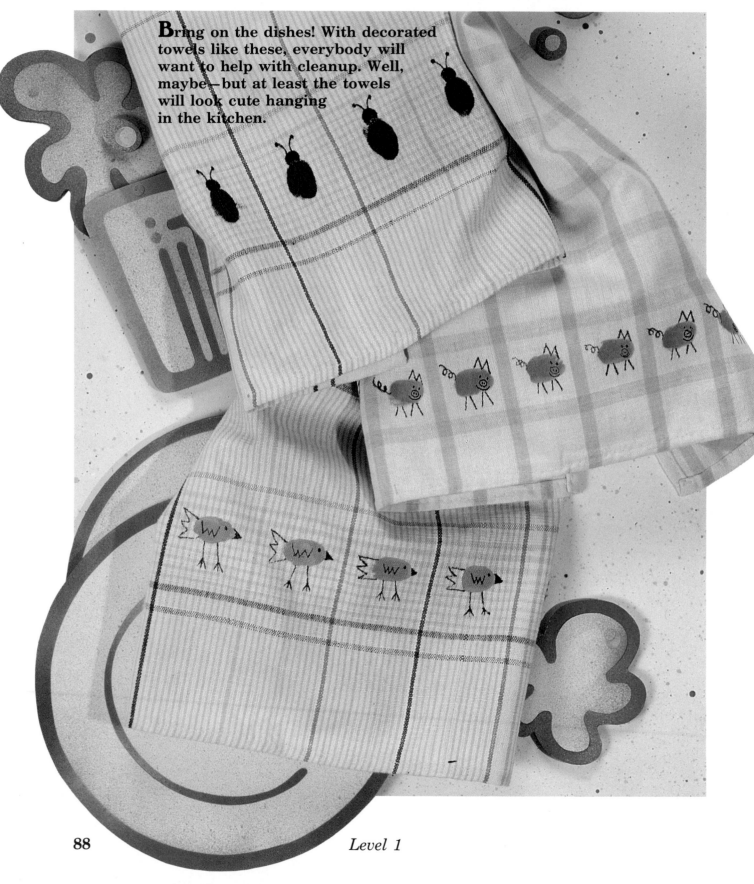

Bring on the dishes! With decorated towels like these, everybody will want to help with cleanup. Well, maybe—but at least the towels will look cute hanging in the kitchen.

Level 1

You will need:
Fabric paints: red, light blue, pink
3 paper plates
3 plaid dishtowels
Fine-point black fabric marker

1. Pour each paint color onto a different paper plate.

2. Unfold the towels and lay them flat. Press your index finger in the paint. Then use your finger like a stamp and stamp 1 oval in each square across 1 end of the towel. (You may want to practice first on paper.) Stamp the same color shape across the other end of the towel. Wash your finger and dry it before changing colors. For the ladybug, use the red paint and make vertical ovals. For the bird, use blue paint and turn your finger sideways to make horizontal ovals. For the pig, use pink paint and make horizontal ovals. Let the paint dry.

3. Use the marker to add the markings on the ladybug's back, head, and antennae. For the pig, draw ears, a tail, legs, and add details to the face. Add a beak, eye, wing, tail, and legs to the bird.

4. To set the paint on the towels, follow the manufacturer's directions.

Paperwhites

It's not a green thumb that's required to cultivate this flower garden—it's planning. The paperwhite bulbs take about four to six weeks to bloom. So "plant" your bulbs just before Thanksgiving and you'll be gathering fragrant flowers just in time for the holidays.

You will need (for each garden):
1 plastic container
Rocks, pebbles, or marbles
5 or 6 paperwhite bulbs
White gift box large enough to hold the
    plastic container
Acrylic paints
Paintbrushes
½ yard of ribbon

1. Fill the container half way with rocks, pebbles, or marbles.

2. Place the bulbs close together on top of the rocks.

3. Place the container in a cold (not freezing!), dark area. Add water to cover the rocks. Leave the container for a couple of weeks, adding more water as it evaporates.

4. When the stems of the bulbs have grown 2″ or 3″ tall, move the container to a bright window that receives indirect sunlight. Continue to add water when needed.

5. When you're ready to give the bulbs away, paint the box. Let it dry. Place the plant container in the box. Tie the ribbon loosely around the stems of the plants.

Squish 'n Wish

Give them to adults to reduce stress. Give them to friends to promote creative thinking, or just give them a squish and make a wish for yourself. Easy to make and fun to give, this is a toy for everyone—above three years of age, that is.

You will need (for each):
A grown-up
Empty 16-ounce plastic shampoo bottle
1 heavy-duty (helium quality latex) 11"
    balloon
½ to ¾ cup of flour
Rag and dishcloth

1. Thoroughly rinse the shampoo bottle
with warm water until all soapsuds are
gone. **Ask the grown-up** to cut off the
bottom of the bottle. Dry the inside of the
bottle thoroughly.

2. Roll down the neck of the balloon and
stretch it over the bottle's neck. Make
sure it fits tightly.

3. Scoop 2 tablespoons of flour into the
bottle and shake the flour into the balloon. Continue adding a tablespoon of
flour at a time until the balloon appears
full. Gently press the balloon against the
countertop to force any air out of the balloon. Add more flour. Continue pressing
out air and filling the balloon with flour
until it's the weight and feel you want.
(The more air inside, the more spongy the
feel. Less air allows the balloon to be
molded into shapes.)

4. When the balloon is filled, pinch it at
the base of the neck and remove the bottle. Tie the neck into a knot. With a
slightly damp rag, wipe off any excess
flour around the outside of the balloon.
Pat the balloon dry with the dishcloth.

Level 2

Parents' Workshop
Great Gifts for Children

St. Nick Apron

When your elf is ready to get cookin', here's an apron that's made to order. It's St. Nick! And he'll keep even the messiest cook under wraps.

You will need:
Tape measure
20″ x 30″ piece of paper (optional)
Ruler (optional)
18″ x 28″ piece of batting
1 yard of red pinwale corduroy
⅓ yard of white pinwale corduroy
3″ x 6″ scrap of pink fabric
Scrap of black fabric
Thread to match fabrics
2 (½″) black buttons
3 (1″) black shank buttons

Note: All seam allowances are ¼″. Prewash the red fabric to prevent the color from running.

1. Measure your elf from neck to knee. At a copy shop, enlarge the pattern as close to this length as possible. (If you enlarge the pattern yourself, draw a grid of 6 squares by 9 squares. For an 18″-long apron, make 2″ squares; 22½″-long apron, 2½″ squares; 27″-long apron, 3″ squares. Transfer the design to your grid square by square.)

2. Add a ¼″ seam allowance around the outer edge of the pattern. Cut it out.

3. Cut 1 St. Nick from the batting and 2 from the red corduroy. (Nap should run the same way on both pieces of corduroy.)

4. From the St. Nick pattern, cut off the top of the hat and the white trim at the bottom of the apron to use as patterns. Cut out the beard/hat trim as 1 piece.

From the white corduroy, cut 1 beard/hat trim, 1 hat top, and 1 bottom trim. (These pieces will already have the ¼″ seam allowances on the sides.)

5. From the St. Nick pattern, carefully cut out the face to use as a pattern. Trace the pattern onto the pink fabric, without adding ¼″ seam allowances. Cut it out.

Cut out the 2 arm semicircles from the St. Nick pattern. Trace the semicircles onto the black fabric and cut them out without adding seam allowances.

6. For the apron front, pin all the pieces in position on 1 St. Nick body. (Refer to the pattern for placement.) Pin the face over the white beard/hat trim piece. Baste the pieces in place. Using white thread, machine-appliqué the white corduroy shapes to the body. (The face will be sewn in place as the hat and beard are appliquéd.) Using black thread, machine-appliqué the 2 black semicircles in place.

7. Baste the batting to the wrong side of the apron front.

8. For the ties, cut 4 (2″ x 25″) strips from the red corduroy. With right sides facing, fold 1 tie in half lengthwise. Sew across 1 end and down the long edge. Turn it right side out; press. Repeat for the other 3 ties. With raw edges aligned, baste the open ends of the ties to the apron front where indicated on the pattern, pinning the rest of the ties out of the way near the center of the body.

9. With right sides facing, pin the apron back to the front. Stitch around the outside edges, leaving about 5″ open on the bottom edge for turning. Trim any excess batting from the seam. Clip the corners and curves slightly. Turn and press.

10. Slipstitch the opening closed. Using red thread, topstitch next to the white zigzag stitching around the hat, beard, and bottom trim. Topstitch ¼″ from the edge of the rest of the body, switching to white thread when stitching over the white corduroy.

11. Sew on the ½″ buttons for the eyes and sew the 1″ buttons on the coat.

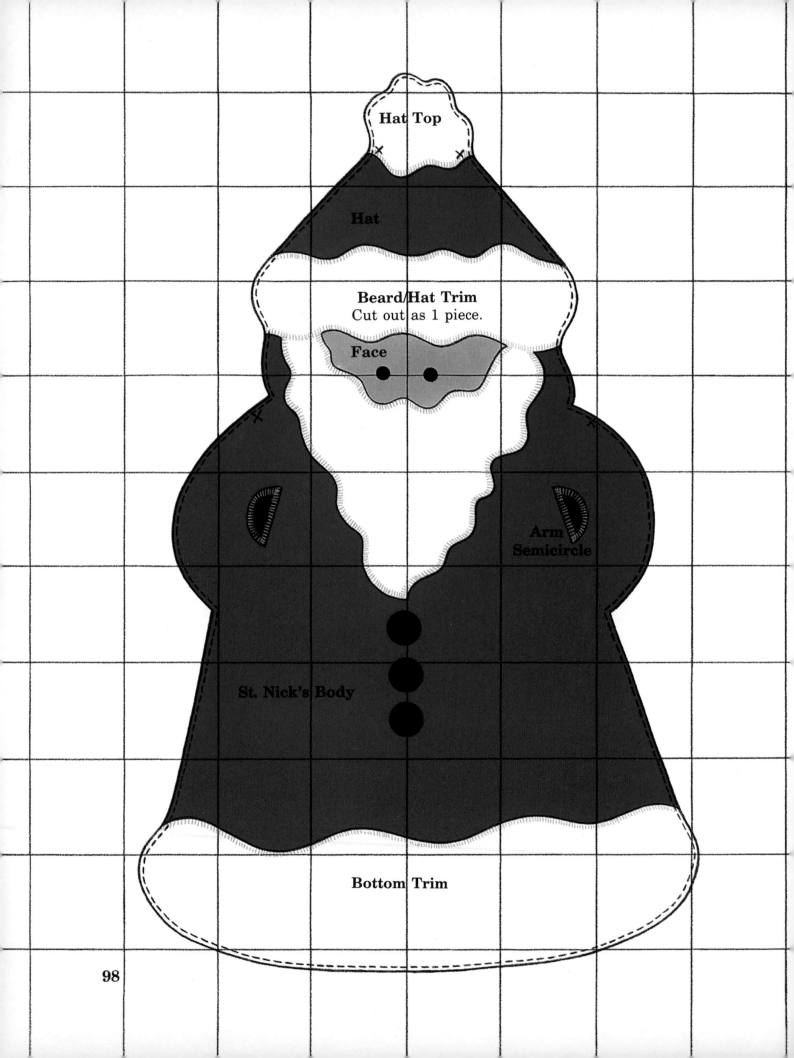

Hat Top

Hat

Beard/Hat Trim
Cut out as 1 piece.

Face

Arm
Semicircle

St. Nick's Body

Bottom Trim

Fleecy  Sweats

Quick and easy, the appliqués for these sweatshirts are cut from Polar Fleece, so the sweatshirts are as comfy as they are cute. This cuddly fabric doesn't ravel, so it's not necessary to turn the edges under—just cut and stitch. These designs were appliquéd by hand using a small hemstitch; but if you're in a real hurry, they may be machine-stitched.

You will need (for 1 sweatshirt):

Tracing paper
Pencil
Scissors
Straight pins
Water-soluble marker
Purchased sweatshirts
Polar Fleece: ⅛ yard of magenta, ⅛ yard of orange, ⅓ yard of bright green
1 small scrap of black felt
Thread to match fabrics

Note: Polar fleece is acrylic. If you need to iron it, be sure to use a pressing cloth as a protective barrier between your iron and the fabric. Direct heat will melt the acrylic fiber.

1. Trace and cut out the patterns as indicated. For the large dinosaur, place the pattern on the fold of the paper. Trace the body. Unfold the paper and trace the head on 1 end and the tail on the other end. Then cut the dinosaur out.

2. Using the water-soluble marker, transfer the patterns to the fleece as indicated and cut them out.

3. Pin the fleece shapes to the sweatshirt, beginning with the large body parts. Wrap the body of the large fish or dinosaur around the side of the sweatshirt to the back. When adding adjacent fleece shapes, be sure that the raw edges of the shapes meet. (See photo.)

4. Using a small hemstitch, securely appliqué the shapes to the sweatshirt. Once the large shapes are sewn in place, add the details such as fins, spikes, and eyes.

5. Pin and appliqué the small fish and baby dinosaur after the large creatures are complete.

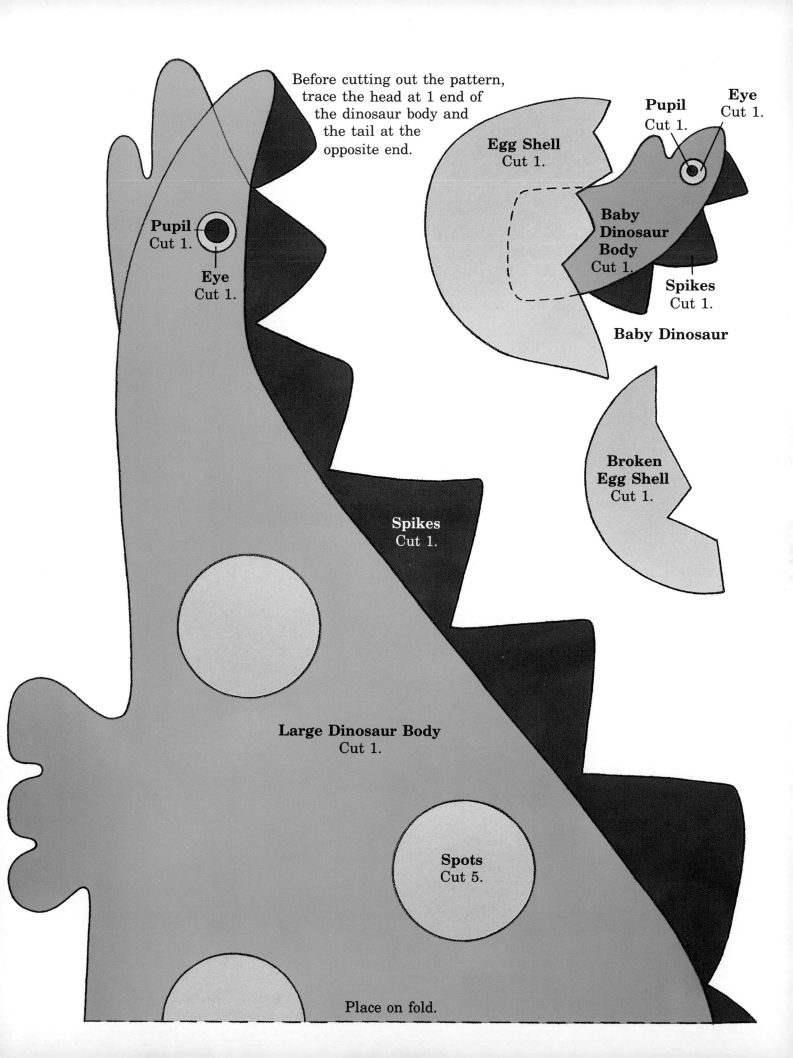

Before cutting out the pattern,
trace the head at 1 end of
the dinosaur body and
the tail at the
opposite end.

Egg Shell
Cut 1.

Pupil
Cut 1.

Eye
Cut 1.

**Baby
Dinosaur
Body**
Cut 1.

Spikes
Cut 1.

Baby Dinosaur

Pupil
Cut 1.

Eye
Cut 1.

**Broken
Egg Shell**
Cut 1.

Spikes
Cut 1.

Large Dinosaur Body
Cut 1.

Spots
Cut 5.

Place on fold.

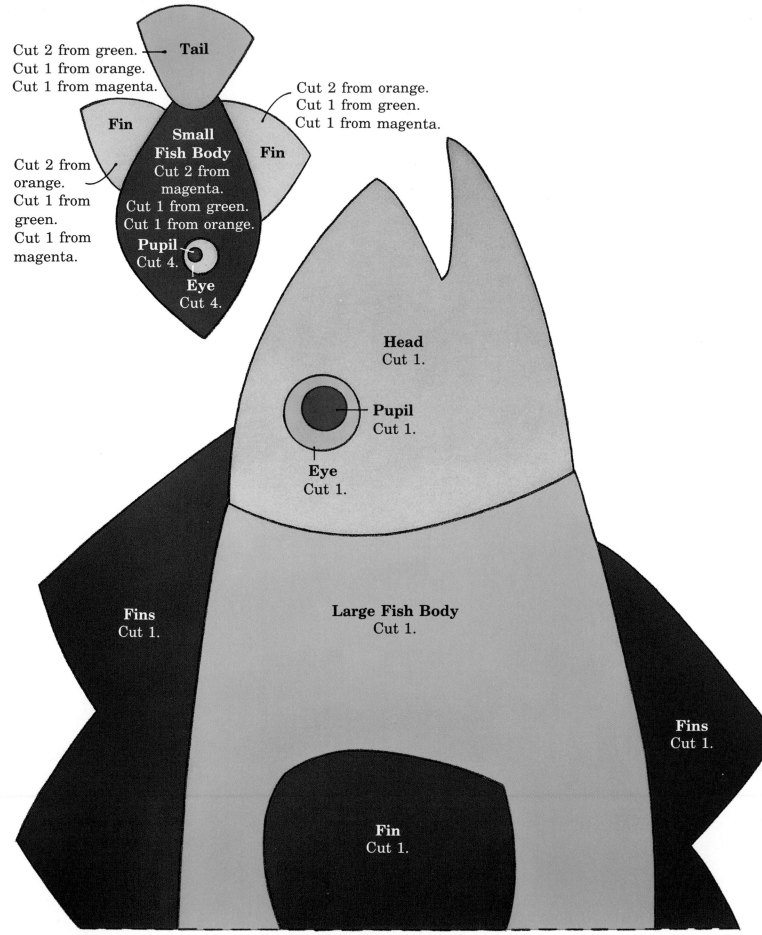

Cut 2 from green.
Cut 1 from orange.
Cut 1 from magenta.

Tail

Cut 2 from orange.
Cut 1 from green.
Cut 1 from magenta.

Fin

Cut 2 from
orange.
Cut 1 from
green.
Cut 1 from
magenta.

Fin

Small Fish Body
Cut 2 from magenta.
Cut 1 from green.
Cut 1 from orange.

Pupil
Cut 4.

Eye
Cut 4.

Head
Cut 1.

Pupil
Cut 1.

Eye
Cut 1.

Fins
Cut 1.

Large Fish Body
Cut 1.

Fins
Cut 1.

Fin
Cut 1.

Match broken lines to complete pattern.

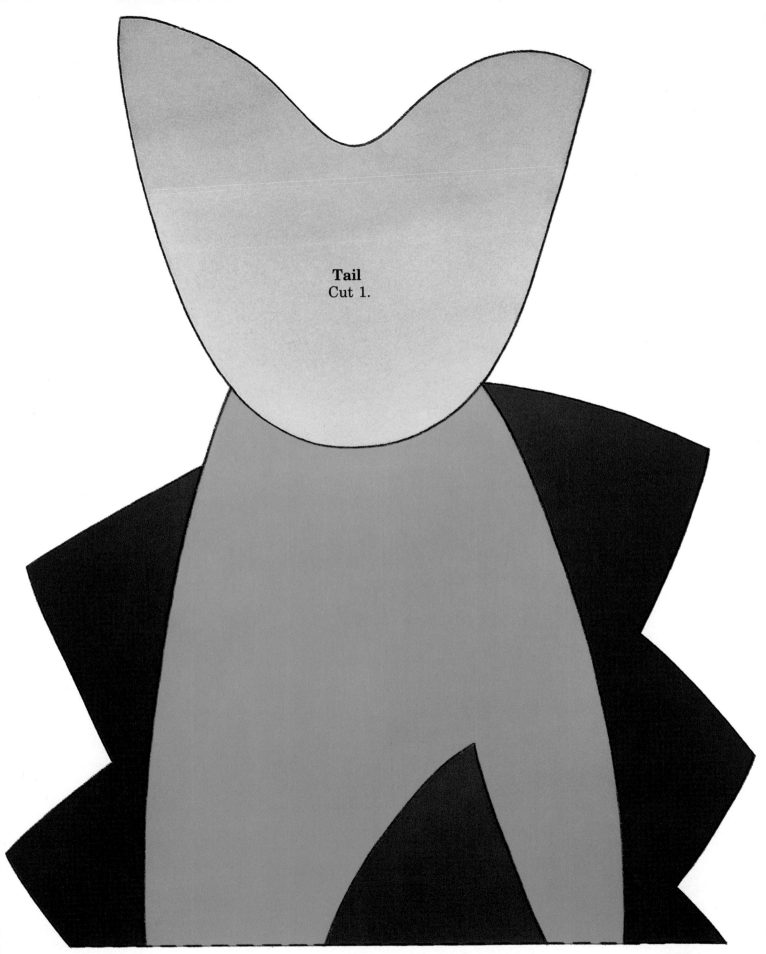

Tail
Cut 1.

Blue-ribbon Boxers

Gather a pair of boxers, a T-shirt, and some colorful ribbons. Then in just a few minutes, you can stitch up these knock-out pj's for your young lady's next round of slumber parties.

You will need (for 1 set of pajamas):

Grosgrain ribbon: 1 yard each of 1½"-wide and 1"-wide; ½ yard each of 1"-wide and ⅝"-wide

Fabric glue

Purchased white T-shirt

Thread to match T-shirt and ribbon

Safety pin

Purchased men's boxer shorts in colors to match the ribbons

1. Cut the 1-yard lengths of ribbon in half.

2. Place these ribbons side by side on the shirt to make a V as shown. Or for a variation, glue the 1"-wide ribbon down the center of the 1½"-wide ribbon.

3. Cut the top ends of the ribbons at an angle to align with the shoulders of the T-shirt. At the center bottom, overlap the ends of the ribbon. Trim any excess to form the point of the V.

4. Glue the ribbons in place. Let them dry.

5. With a top thread that matches the ribbon and white bobbin thread, topstitch the ribbons in place along each long edge.

Zigzag-stitch the cut ends of the ribbons at the shoulder seams and at the center bottom.

6. Cut a 1" piece from the ⅝"-wide ribbon. Then make a bow using the remaining lengths of ribbon. Wrap the center of the bow with the 1" piece of ribbon. Slipstitch the ends together to secure the bow.

7. With the safety pin, pin the bow in place at the bottom of the V. Remove the bow before laundering.

8. If the waist in the boxers is too large, sew a tuck in the waistband.

105

Belly Bags

Whether climbing the Rockies or scaling the heights in their own backyard, little explorers need a place to store their compasses and stash their cookies. With these Belly Bags, the adventurers will know their gear is close at hand.

You will need (for 1 bag):
Tracing paper
Pencil
Scissors
Straight pins
Needle
Water-soluble fabric marker
½ yard of paper-backed fusible web
12″ square of muslin
6″ x 12″ piece of fleece
For the raccoon: ⅓ yard of yellow nylon fabric, scraps of teal nylon, teal thread, 2 (⅜″) sew-on wiggle eyes, purple fanny pack
For the beaver: ⅓ yard of pink nylon, scraps of orange nylon, pink thread, 2 (⅜″) sew-on wiggle eyes, red fanny pack
For the snail: ⅓ yard of orange nylon, scraps of teal nylon, teal and yellow thread, 1 (⅜″) sew-on wiggle eye, blue fanny pack

1. Trace and cut out the desired animal patterns.

2. From the ⅓ yard of fabric, cut a 12″ square. Using the water-soluble marker, transfer the animal's outline to the right side of the fabric, ½″ from the bottom edge.

3. Following the manufacturer's instructions, fuse the paper-backed web to the wrong side of the scraps of fabric needed for the decorative details. For the raccoon, fuse the fabric for the eyes, nose, and tail stripes. For the beaver, fuse the fabrics for the nose, ears, and tail. Transfer the patterns to the fabrics and cut out the shapes. Fuse the shapes in place on the right side of the animal outline.

4. Fuse the muslin to the wrong side of the decorated square.

5. Fold the square in half, wrong sides facing, and sandwich the fleece between. Pin and then baste the layers together.

6. Using a medium satin-stitch, machine-appliqué the small shapes first and then outline the main shapes as shown on the pattern. Cut out the animals close to the stitching. Satin-stitch the outer edges of the shapes again with a slightly wider setting to fill in the stitches and cover the raw edges.

7. With matching thread, hand-sew the wiggle eyes in place.

8. Unzip the bag. Pin the center of the animal to the top layer only at the center front of the bag. Topstitch around the sides and bottom of the animal as indicated on the pattern, leaving an opening between the Xs to create another pocket.

Topstitch around the animals, leaving the area between the Xs unstitched to create another pocket.

Raccoon

Snail

Beaver

109

Novelty Knits

Add dots and dashes or little bows with duplicate stitching to brighten plain purchased knits. With this stitch, you can quickly create novelty hats and mittens to coordinate with winter jackets and coats.

You will need:
Purchased knitted mittens and hat with a gauge of 6 to 8 stitches and 8 to 10 rows per 1″
1 roll of contrasting punch-embroidery yarn
Tapestry needle

For Bows and Stripes

1. Thread the needle with 1 doubled strand or 2 single strands of yarn. For the mittens, follow the chart and begin duplicate-stitching the bow at the center of the back of 1 mitten. (Figures A and B.) Then stitch a stripe all the way around the mitten, 1″ above the bow. Stitch another stripe 1″ below the bow. Duplicate-stitch the second mitten in the same way.

2. For the hat, stitch 2 horizontal stripes around the cuff, ¼″ from the top and ¼″ from the bottom edge.

Duplicate Stitch
Figure A

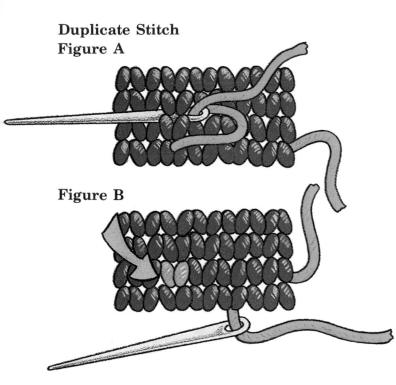

Figure B

For Stripes and Dots

1. Thread the needle with 1 doubled strand or 2 single strands of yarn. For the striped mitten, begin duplicate-stitching the middle stripe on 1 side of the mitten. Continue stitching all the way around. Then stitch stripes ½″ above and ½″ below the middle stripe. Stitch a stripe around the thumb that corresponds to the middle stripe.

2. On the back of the other mitten, randomly stitch small, medium, and large dots as desired. On the palm of the mitten, stitch 1 medium dot.

3. For the hat, randomly stitch small, medium, and large dots on the top section of the hat. Stitch vertical rows of stripes along the cuff about 1½″ apart.

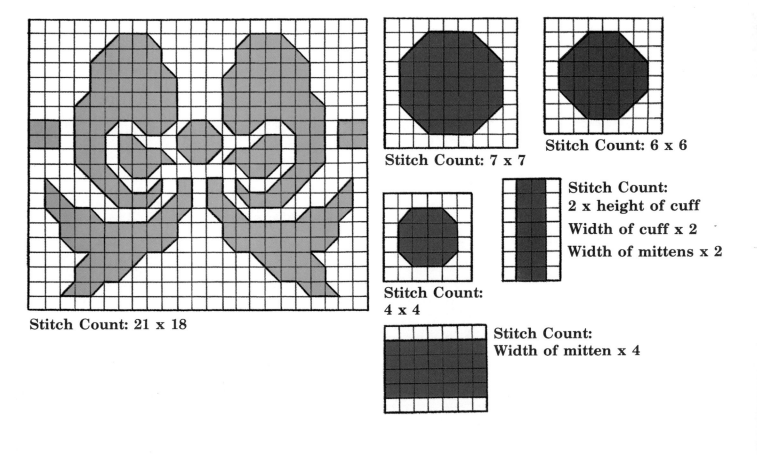

Stitch Count: 21 x 18

Stitch Count: 7 x 7

Stitch Count: 6 x 6

Stitch Count: 4 x 4

Stitch Count: 2 x height of cuff

Width of cuff x 2

Width of mittens x 2

Stitch Count: Width of mitten x 4

Reindeer Collar

Let the party season begin! Your little guy will be right in style for any holiday happening wearing this removable appliquéd collar. Shown here worn over a purchased shirt and shortalls, the red-nosed reindeer greets the season with a smile.

You will need (for 1 collar):
½ yard (45″-wide) white-on-white pincord or white piqué
½ yard (45″-wide) white batiste for lining
White thread
2 elastic loops
Paper-backed fusible web
Scraps of fabric: light brown, dark brown, white, red
Thread to match
2 yards of red piping
⅝ yard (¾″-wide) Christmas ribbon
Liquid ravel preventer
Safety pin
½ yard (⅛″-wide) white ribbon

Note: The collar patterns include ½″ seam allowances.

1. Trace and transfer all the patterns and markings.

2. Place the collar pattern on the fold of the collar fabric and cut it out, marking the center front. Repeat for the lining.

3. With the raw edges aligned, pin the ends of 1 elastic loop to the right side of the collar at the top center back (the loop will face to the inside). Stitch securely. Repeat with the second loop on the opposite side of the collar back.

4. Following the manufacturer's instructions, fuse the web to the wrong side of the fabric scraps. Pin all of the appliqué patterns to the right side of the fabric scraps and cut them out. Remove the paper backing from the back of the appliqué shapes.

5. Fuse the reindeer's head in place on the center front of the collar. Fuse the antlers and then the eyes and nose in place.

6. Before stitching around the appliqué shapes, slide a piece of paper under the collar for stability. With the matching thread, machine-appliqué the reindeer's head through the paper. Stitch again for a smoother edge. Machine-appliqué the antlers, the eyes, and the nose in the same manner. Satin-stitch the mouth red and the pupils of the eyes black. Tear away the paper and press the appliqué.

7. With right sides facing and raw edges aligned, stitch the piping to the collar along the outside edges, beginning and ending at the elastic loops.

8. With right sides facing and raw edges aligned, stitch the collar and the lining together, leaving 1½″ open on 1 side. Trim seams to ¼″ and clip the curves and corners. Turn the collar right side out and press. Slipstitch the opening closed.

9. Tie a bow with the Christmas ribbon and notch the ends. Apply liquid ravel preventer to the ribbon ends. Safety-pin the bow to the center front of the collar just below the reindeer.

10. To secure the collar around the neck, thread the white ribbon through the 2 elastic loops and tie it in a bow.

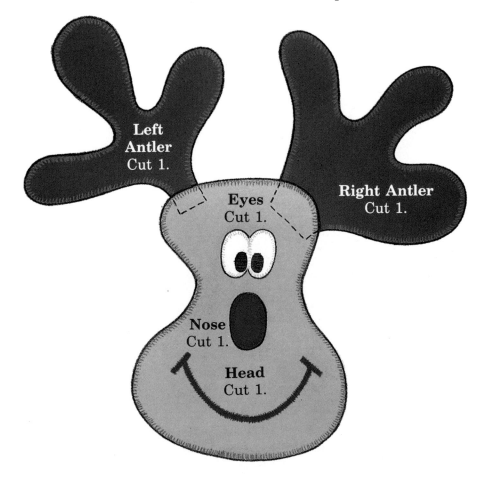

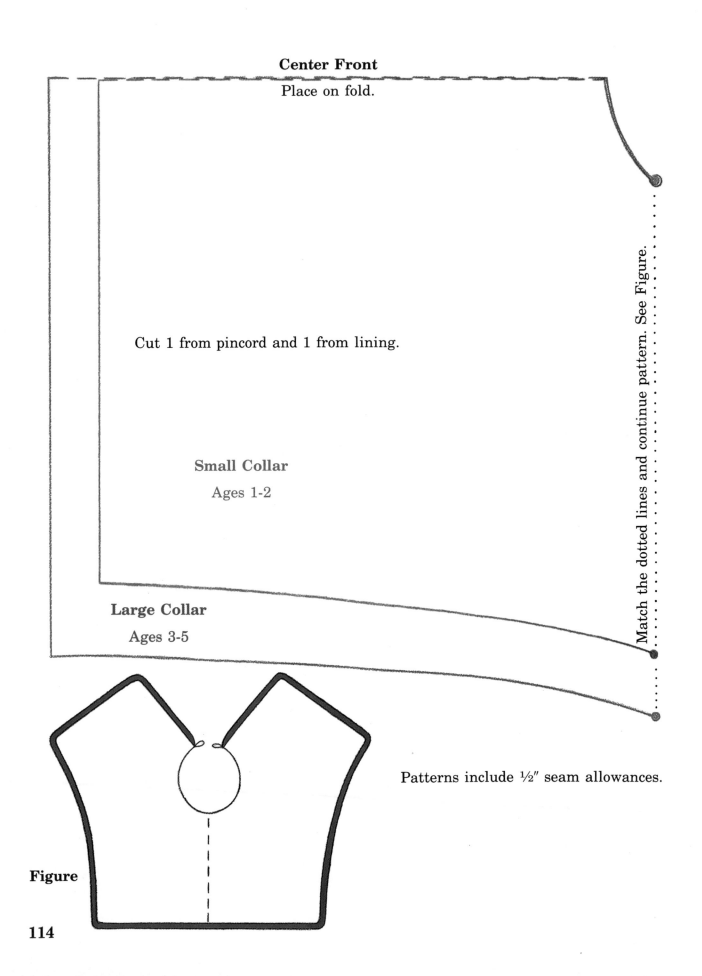

Center Front

Place on fold.

Cut 1 from pincord and 1 from lining.

Small Collar

Ages 1-2

Large Collar

Ages 3-5

Match the dotted lines and continue pattern. See Figure.

Patterns include ½″ seam allowances.

Figure

114

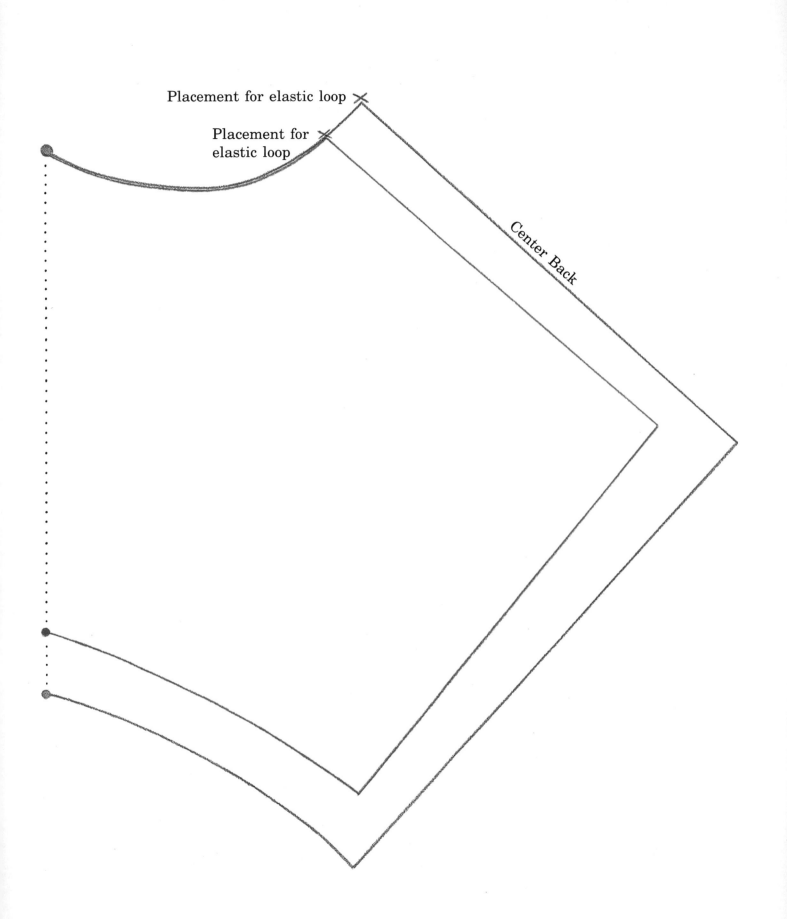

Placement for elastic loop ✕

Placement for elastic loop ✕

Center Back

115

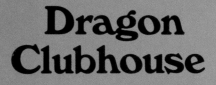

Dragon
Clubhouse

Just for Fun

DON'T
FEED
DRAGON

Rainy days don't have to drag on—not if you have a dragon in the garage! Made out of cardboard boxes gathered from an appliance store and a moving company, this dragon is big enough for little knights to climb inside and while away the day. Each section is made separately and stacks together to form this mythical monster.

You will need:
Hot-glue gun and glue sticks
3 (18″ x 18″ x 24″) dish barrel boxes
Yardstick
Pencil
Carpet knife and blades
2 (3″ x 5″) cardboard cylinders
1 empty paper towel roll
2 same-size refrigerator boxes
Masking tape
1 (9″ x 12″ x 4″) shoe box
12-ounce cans of acrylic spray paint: 4 green, 4 yellow, 1 red, 1 orange, 1 fuchsia
2 yellow tennis balls

Making the Head

1. Glue 1 end of 1 dish barrel box closed. Let the glue dry.

Place the box on its side with the open end pointing to the right. On the edge of the box, measure and mark 10″ from the upper left corner. Draw a line from this point along the edge to the open end of the box. Measure and mark 8″ above the lower right corner of the box along the flap fold line. Draw a line from this point to the bottom edge of the box. Draw a diagonal line connecting the 10″ and 8″ marks. (Figure A.)

Mark the opposite side of the box to match. Draw a line across the top of the box connecting the 10″ marks.

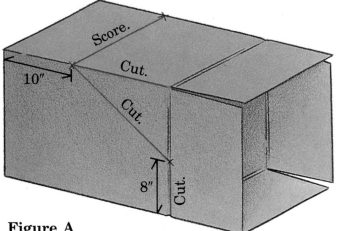

Figure A

2. Using the carpet knife, score the line across the top of the box. Cut through the cardboard on all the other lines.

3. Fold the top section down along the score line so that the cut edges meet. (Figure B.) Make a mark on the top edge of the box where it meets the 8″ mark. Make a mark at the same point on the opposite edge and draw a line across the box to connect the 2 marks. Score this line. Fold the cardboard down along the score line. Fold up the lower flap and trim it to meet the score line of the top flap. Using a generous amount of glue, hot-glue the cut edges and flaps in place. Let the glue dry.

4. Draw a 12″-diameter circle in the center bottom of the head box. Cut it out.

Figure B

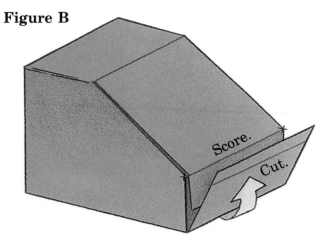

5. Trace and cut out the mouth pattern. Center the pattern on the glued flap section of the head and trace around it. Cut it out.

6. To make a nostril, cut out the bottom of 1 cylinder. Make 2 marks 1″ apart and ½″ below the edge of the top rim of the cylinder. (Figure C.) Connect the 2 marks. Make 2 marks 1″ apart along the bottom rim of the cylinder directly opposite the first marks. Draw a line from each top mark around the cylinder to each bottom mark. Cut along the lines. Repeat to make the second nostril.

Figure C

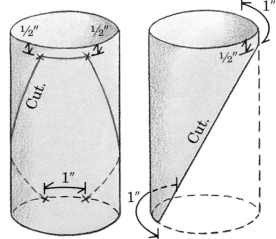

7. Trace and cut out the flame pattern. Cut 2 flames from cardboard scraps. To make the horns, split the seams on the paper towel roll to form 2 spirals. Set these aside.

Making the Body

1. Place 1 refrigerator box on its side. Using the carpet knife, cut the seam that runs the length of the box. Place the open box on the floor with the writing facing up. On 1 end, trim the flaps so that they each measure 3½″ wide. Cut off the flaps on the opposite end.

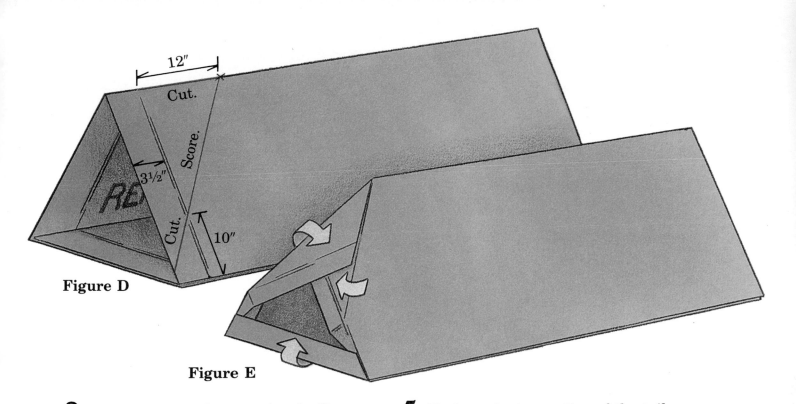

12″

Cut.

Score.

3½″

Cut.

10″

Figure D

Figure E

2. Fold the box to form a triangle. Turn the triangle so that the overlapping sides are on the bottom. Hot-glue and tape the sides together. (Figure D.)

3. At the end of the box with the flaps, mark as shown in Figure D. Repeat on the other side of the same end of the box.

4. Using the knife, cut on the 12″ line. Score on the diagonal lines. Cut the line that extends into the flap area. Fold the side flaps in. (Figure E.) Then fold the cardboard down on the score lines and glue the edges to the side flaps. Fold the bottom flap up and glue it in place.

5. To form the top section of the tail on the opposite end of the box, draw a 24″-long line from the peak toward the center of the box. Mark this point. (Figure F.) Then measure 24″ up from the bottom right corner and mark. Connect these 2 marks. Repeat from the bottom left corner. To make a tab for gluing, draw a second line 2″ above and parallel to this one.

6. Using the knife, cut along the top 24″ line and the line on the right side. On the left side, cut the top line and score the line below. Align the right cut side with the score line on the left. Glue the left flap under the right side. Tape along the top where the sides meet.

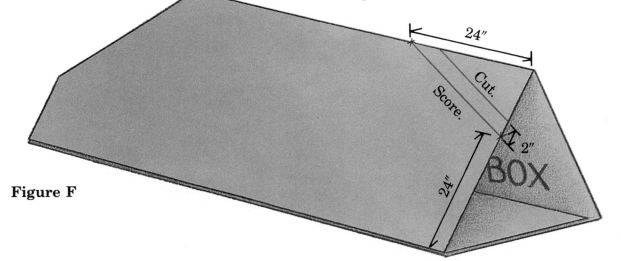

24″

Cut.

Score.

2″

24″

BOX

Figure F

119

Figure G

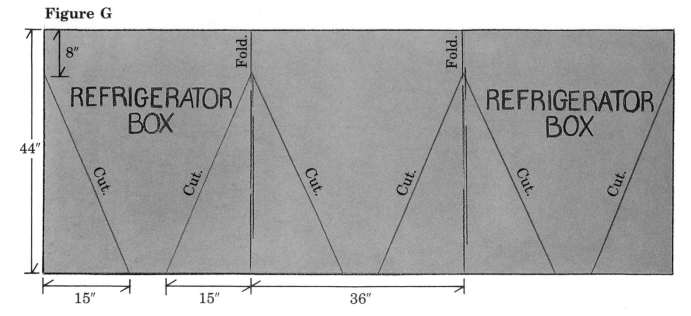

REFRIGERATOR BOX   Fold.   REFRIGERATOR BOX   Fold.

8"

44"

Cut. Cut. Cut. Cut. Cut. Cut.

15"   15"   36"

Making the Tail

1. Place the second refrigerator box on its side. Cut the seam that runs the length of the box. Place the open box on the floor with the writing facing up. Cut off the flaps. Cut the box so that it is 3 sections wide and 44" long.

2. Mark each section as shown in Figure G. Cut along the marked lines. Fold the sections to form a triangle. Glue and tape the triangle together along the cut edges.

3. For a spine pattern, draw an 11" x 8" x 8" triangle. Add 2" to the 11" base for a glue flap. Trace and cut out 9 spines from cardboard scraps. Score the 11" base lines.

Making the Legs

1. For the back legs, place a dish barrel box on its side. Cut on the seam that runs the length of the box. Open the box and cut off 2 sections. (You will need 1 section for each leg.) Cut off the flap on 1 end of each section.

2. Measure 11" from the bottom right corner (excluding the flap which will go under the dragon) of 1 section and make a mark. (Figure H.) Make a second mark 4" above this one.

Figure H

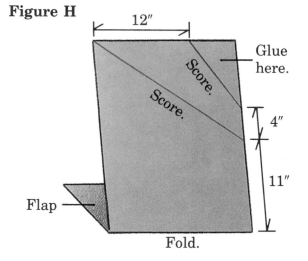

12"

Glue here.

Score.

Score.

4"

11"

Flap

Fold.

From the upper left corner, measure 12" and mark. Draw a line from the 12" mark to the 4" mark. Draw a line from the upper left corner to the 11" mark. Score along these lines. Bend the cardboard on the score lines to form the leg. Repeat for the second back leg. Glue the legs to the dragon. (See photo.)

3. For the front legs, glue the edges of the lid inside the shoe box so there isn't a ridge. Draw a diagonal line from the lower left corner to the upper right corner and continue around the box. (Figure I.) Cut the box in half along this line. Glue the front legs to the dragon. (See photo.)

Figure I

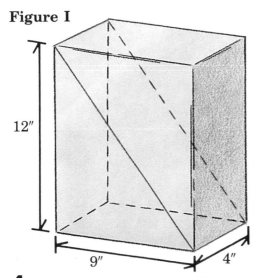

12″
9″
4″

4. For the claws, trace and cut out the patterns. Cut 2 front claws and 2 back claws. Set them aside.

Making the Neck

1. For the neck, glue the flaps down on 1 end of a dish barrel box. Let the glue dry. Draw a 12″-diameter circle in the center of this end. Cut it out.

2. On the opposite end of the box, cut off the flaps. Find the center on 1 lower edge on this end of the box. Measure 12″ above this point and mark. Draw a line from this mark to the lower right and left corners. Do the same on the opposite side of the box. Cut the cardboard on these lines. Place the neck on the body. (See photo.) Trace around the outside of the neck onto the body. Remove the neck and draw a second line 1″ inside the first. Cut an opening in the body on the inside line.

Painting the Dragon

1. Paint the head, neck, tail, legs, and body green. Let dry. For a mottled look, spray yellow paint randomly over the green.

2. Paint the inside of the nostrils red and the outside green.

3. To paint the eyes, cut a 4″ square from a scrap of cardboard. Transfer the circle pattern to the cardboard and cut it out to make a stencil. Place the stencil against 1 tennis ball, making sure the cutout area isn't on the seam of the ball. Paint the circle red. Paint the second ball the same way.

4. Paint the claws and flames red. Paint the horns fushia. Paint the spines different colors.

Assembling the Dragon

1. To assemble the head, measure and mark the placement for 1 eye 6″ from the top of the head and 5½″ from 1 side. Center the circle stencil over the mark and trace around it. Cut the circle out. Repeat for the other eye on the other side of the head.

For the placement of the nostrils, measure and mark 5½″ below the center of each eye circle. Glue the eyes inside the cutout holes. Glue the nostrils in place.

Tape the flames to the inside of the mouth. Glue the horns to the top of the head. (See photo.)

2. Glue the front claws to the top edge of the front legs. Glue the back claws to the lower side of the back legs.

3. Place the neck over the cutout area on the back of the body. Stack the head on top of the neck.

4. Slip the large end of the tail over the rear of the body. Glue the spines in place down the back of the body and tail.

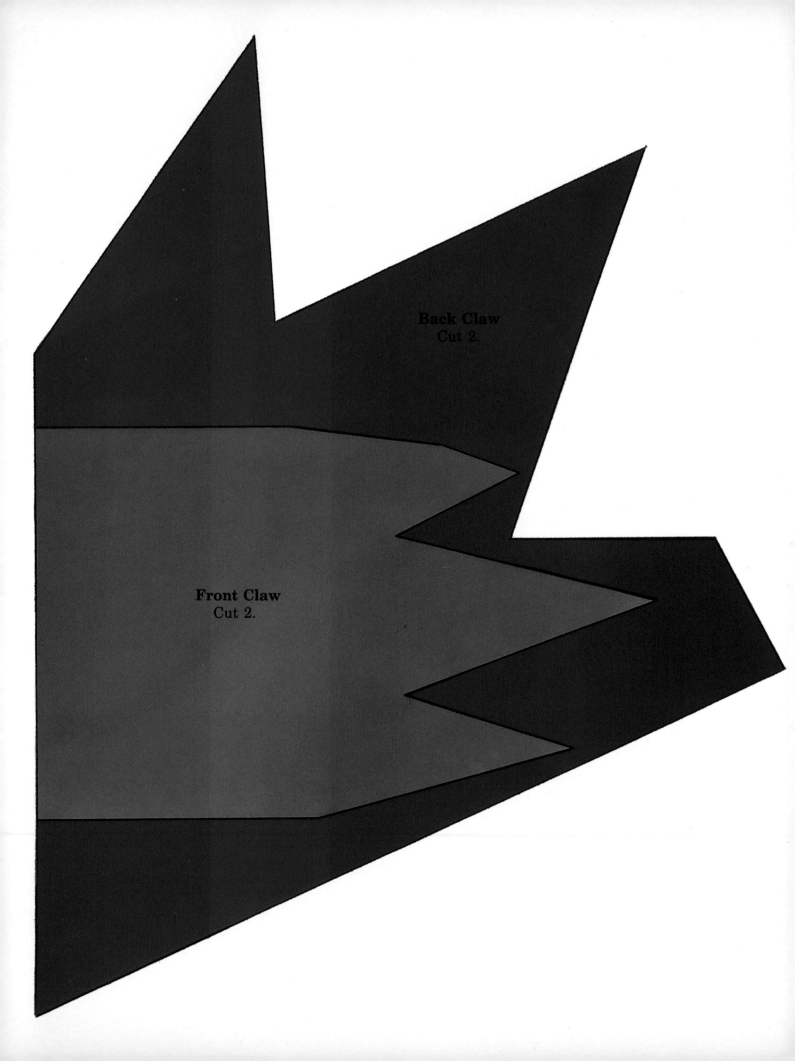

Back Claw
Cut 2.

Front Claw
Cut 2.

You will need:

Tracing paper
Scraps of ¾″ plywood
Scraps of ¼″ plywood
Saber saw or coping saw
Wooden dowels: 1 (⅜″ x 34″), 1 (¼″ x 7″)
Awl
Electric drill with ³⁄₃₂″, ¹⁄₁₆″, ¼″, ⅜″ bits,
  and ⁵⁄₁₆″ spade bit
3 (¼″) screw eyes
Sandpaper
1½″-wide masking tape
Acrylic paints: red, yellow, blue, pink
Paintbrushes
Wood glue
1¾ yards of thin cord for fishing line

Making the Pole

1. Trace and cut out all the patterns.

2. Trace the rod handle and reel body patterns onto the ¾″ plywood. Trace the fish, spool ends, and crank patterns on the ¼″ plywood. Using the saber saw, cut out all the shapes.

3. From the ¼″ dowel, cut a 5″ length and a 1¼″ length.

4. With the ⅜″ bit, drill a hole in the center of the squared end of the handle. (See pattern.) Using the spade bit, drill holes in the reel body, drilling straight through both sides and making sure the holes stay aligned. (Figure A.)

5. To make holes for the screw eyes, pierce holes with the awl on the long dowel at the center, ¼″ from 1 end, and 3½″ from the other end. With the awl, pierce the 5″ dowel 1½″ from 1 end; then drill a ³⁄₃₂″ hole through the dowel at this point to provide an anchor for the fishing line. Using the ¼″ bit, drill a hole all the

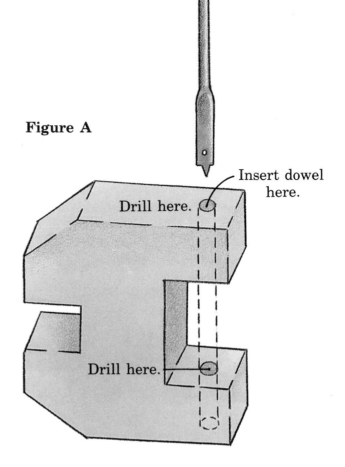

Figure A

way through the fish for the eye. Use the same bit to drill holes in the center of each spool end. Using the ¹⁄₁₆″ bit, drill a hole all the way through the fish's mouth where indicated on the pattern.

6. Sand all the pieces smooth.

7. Paint the rod and reel as follows, letting each color dry before adding another. Paint the long dowel yellow. For the red stripes, wrap the dowel with the masking tape in a candy cane pattern; then paint the untaped area red. When the paint is dry, remove the tape. Paint the rod handle red. Paint the crank yellow. Paint the reel body blue. Then paint yellow stripes all around the edges of the reel. Paint the edges of spool ends pink. Paint the fish as indicated on the pattern.

8. After the paint is completely dry, paint all pieces with several coats of clear enamel, allowing the enamel to dry between coats.

Assembling the Pole

1. To attach the crank handle to the reel, slide the end of the 5″-long dowel closest to the anchor hole through 1 of the holes in the reel. Slip both of the spool ends onto the dowel and continue sliding the dowel through the other hole in the reel. Slide the spools to the opposite sides of the opening in the reel. (Figure B.) Glue the crank to the other end of the dowel as shown. Glue the 1¼″-long dowel in the hole on the opposite end of the crank.

2. Apply glue to the edges of the handle notch on the reel body. Insert the handle into the notch 1″ from the square end, with the crank on the left side of the rod handle for a left-handed fisherman or on the right side of the handle for a right-handed one. Let the glue dry.

3. Insert the screw eyes into the holes in the long dowel. Glue the end of the dowel without the screw eyes into the hole in the rod handle, positioning the screw eyes on top. (Figure C.) Let the glue dry.

4. Thread 1 end of the cord through the anchor hole in the center of the reel dowel and tie a knot. Thread the remaining cord through the screw eyes to the end of the rod and through the hole in the fish's mouth. Tie the end in a knot. Reel the excess cord onto the reel.

Figure B

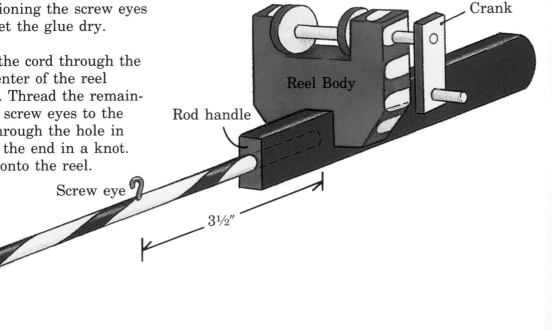

Figure C

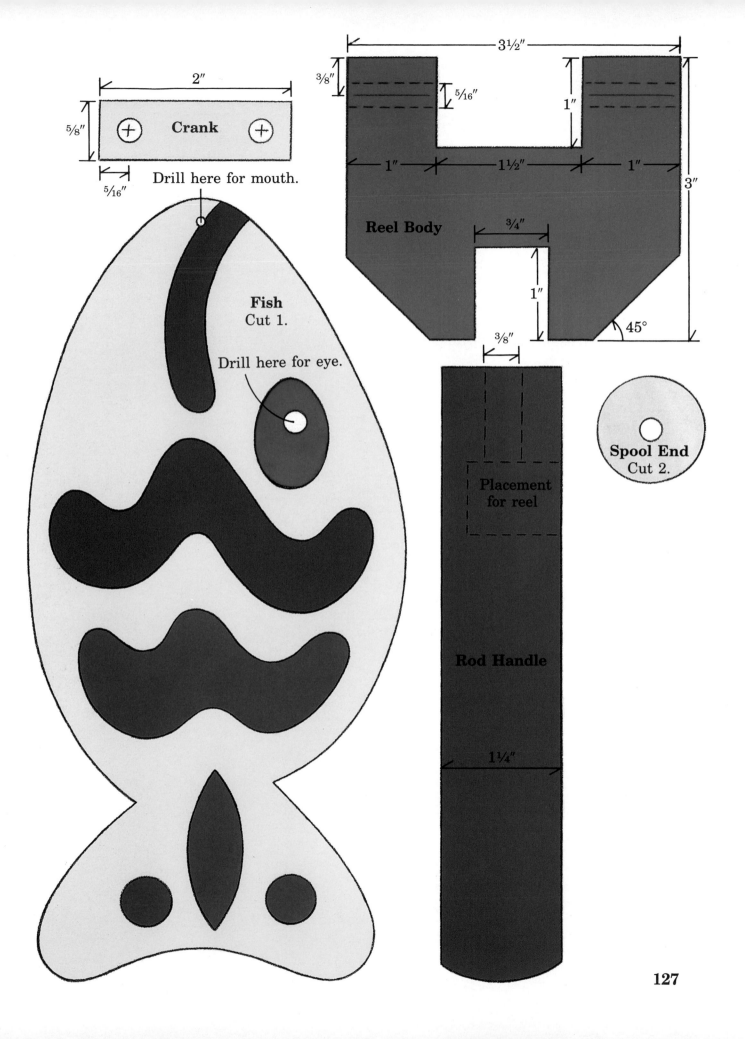

2"

Crank

⁵⁄₈"

⁵⁄₁₆"

Drill here for mouth.

3½"

³⁄₈"

⁵⁄₁₆"

1"

1"

1½"

1"

3"

Reel Body

³⁄₄"

1"

45°

³⁄₈"

Fish
Cut 1.

Drill here for eye.

Placement
for reel

Rod Handle

1¼"

Spool End
Cut 2.

127

Baseball Card Catcher

Hit a homerun with your baseball fan by stitching this nifty pouch. With fifty-six individual pockets, there's lots of room for organizing a card collection in time for spring training.

You will need:
1 yard of clear vinyl
3 yards of extra-wide white bias tape
White thread
36″ x 25″ piece of heavyweight green
   fabric
Masking tape
31½″ (⅜″-diameter) wooden dowel
Yellow spray paint
2 baseballs
Electric drill with ⅜″ bit
7 (¾″) white star appliqués
Fabric glue
1 yard of monofilament

1. Cut the vinyl into 8 (4″ x 25″) strips. Cut the bias tape into 2 (36″) pieces and 1 (26″) piece.

2. Place a vinyl strip across the bottom short end of the fabric. Use the tape to hold it in place temporarily. Zigzag-stitch along the bottom edge of the vinyl. Remove the tape. Tape a second vinyl strip right above the top edge of the first strip. Zigzag-stitch along the bottom edge of second strip, keeping the top edge of the previous strip open. Add the next 6 strips the same way.

3. To make the pockets, measure 3½″ from 1 long edge of the fabric and draw a vertical line the length of the fabric. Measure 3½″ from this line and draw another line. Continue across the fabric until you have drawn 6 lines. Straightstitch down each line.

4. To bind the edges, fold 1 (36″) piece of bias tape in half over 1 long edge of the fabric and stitch it in place. Repeat with the second 36″ piece on the opposite long edge. Place the 26″ bias strip over the bottom edge, covering the edge of the bottom vinyl strip. Fold the ends under and stitch it in place.

5. To make a casing for the dowel, fold under ½″ on the top edge of the fabric. Fold under another 1″ and press. Stitch along the first folded edge.

6. Paint the dowel yellow and let it dry.

7. Drill a ½″-deep hole in the center of each baseball.

8. Glue the white stars on the casing, centering 1 star over each vertical row of pockets.

9. Slip the dowel through the casing; press a baseball onto each end. For a hanger, tie each end of the monofilament to the dowel next to the baseballs.

A Magical Mount

Transporting your prince or princess to an enchanted land is an easy task for this unicorn. He's always ready to whisk young royalty from one fairy-tale adventure to another.

You will need:

Tracing paper
Pencil
Scissors
Water-soluble marker
1 yard of 45″-wide cotton fabric and
    matching thread
Acrylic paints: gold, blue
Paintbrushes
Liquid ravel preventer
Polyester stuffing
Sandpaper: coarse and fine
Wooden dowels: 1 (1″ x 12″), 1 (1″ x 36″)
Clear acrylic spray
Electric drill with ¼″ and ½″ bits
Handsaw
⅜″ chisel
1 (#8) 1″-long flathead screw
Screwdriver
12″ length of 1 x 6 pine
1 (¼″-diameter) 2½″-long screw-top bolt
    with nut
6 washers
Craft glue
2 (54″-long) red shoestrings
Crewel needle
2 (½″) gold star buttons
2 (¾″) black buttons
12 yards (⅜″-wide) yellow ribbon and
    matching thread

Making the Unicorn

1. Enlarge the patterns and add ¼″ seam allowances. Cut out the patterns. Using the water soluble-marker, transfer the patterns and markings to the fabric. Cut them out.

2. Paint the squares around the eyes and nose gold. Let them dry.

3. Cut out the circle on each side of the head. (This is where you'll insert the 12″ dowel handle.) Apply liquid ravel preventer to the raw edges. Let it dry.

4. With right sides facing and raw edges aligned, sew the gusset to 1 side of the head, aligning the dots at the throat and the nose. Sew the other side of the gusset to the second head piece in the same way.

5. With right sides facing, sew the remaining seams of the 2 head pieces together, leaving the bottom open. Clip the curves and turn the head right side out.

6. With right sides facing, sew the horn pieces together, leaving the bottom open. Clip the curve and turn it right side out. Press the bottom edge under ¼″. Stuff the horn firmly. Pin the horn to the head where indicated on the pattern and slip-stitch it securely in place.

7. To make 1 ear, place 2 ear pieces together with right sides facing. Stitch along the outside edges, leaving a 3″ opening at the bottom for turning. Trim the corners, turn, and press. Blindstitch the opening closed. Run a gathering thread around the entire base of the ear. Pull to gather tightly and secure the thread. Fold the ear in half and stitch it to the head where indicated.

Making the Base and Handles

1. Beginning with the coarse sandpaper and finishing with the fine, sand both dowels so that the ends are rounded and the entire surface is smooth for painting. Paint the dowels gold to match the squares on the face. (This may require several coats.) Let the paint dry between coats. Then apply several coats of the acrylic spray, letting it dry between coats.

2. Drill a hole through the center of the 12″ dowel handle, using the ¼″ bit. In the 36″ dowel, use the handsaw and the chisel to cut out a notch 3″ from 1 end. (Figure

Figure A

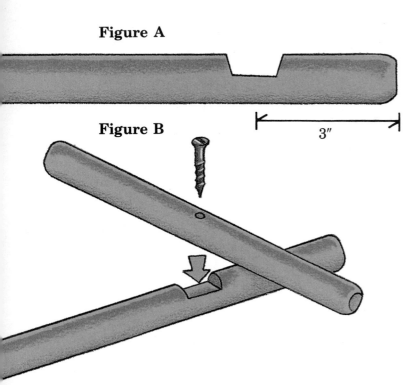

Figure B

3″

A.) Fit the dowel handle in the notch, with the hole centered and the handle perpendicular to long dowel. Screw the handle in place to secure it. (Figure B.)

3. Trace the wheel pattern and cut it out. Transfer the pattern and details to the 1 x 6 pine 2 times. Using the electric drill and ½″ bit, drill a hole through the center of each wheel. Cut out the wheels. Sand them smooth. Paint the wheels blue. Apply several coats of paint, letting the paint dry between coats.

4. To attach the wheels to the 36″ dowel, use the ¼″ bit to drill a hole through the dowel, about 1″ from the bottom.

5. Slip the bolt through 1 wheel. Then slip on 3 washers. Slip the bolt through the dowel. Slip 3 more washers onto the bolt and then add the second wheel. Secure the bolt with the nut. Tighten the nut until the wheels rotate freely but don't wobble.

Assembling the Unicorn

1. Place the handle into the unicorn head, slipping the handles through the cutout circles. Stuff the head firmly, especially around and above the dowels. Poke in the fabric around the handles and glue it in place.

2. Turn the bottom hem under ¼″. Turn it up again on the fold line. (See pattern.) Sew the hem in place, gathering it tightly around the dowel. Glue the gathers to the dowel at the tie line. Wrap 1 shoestring around the gathers and tie it in a bow.

3. For the bridle, fold the other shoestring in half and wrap it around the nose. Tack it in place under the chin, leaving long tails. Bring the shoestring tails over the handles and knot the ends together at the back of the head.

4. Thread the crewel needle with 4 strands of thread. Sew the star buttons in place on each side of the nose to secure the bridle. Sew the buttons in place for eyes where indicated on the pattern.

5. To make the unicorn's mane, use the yellow ribbon to make a 3″ loop. Slipstitch the loop in place 2″ behind the horn on the seam. (Figure C.) Continue making and stitching loops 6″ down the back of the head.

Figure C

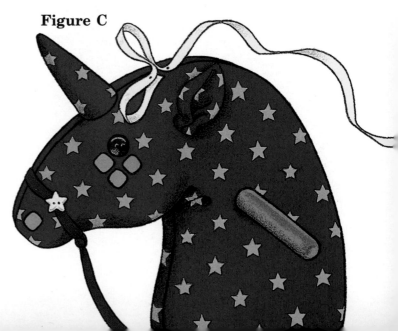

Enlarge each square to equal 1″ or photocopy at 166%.

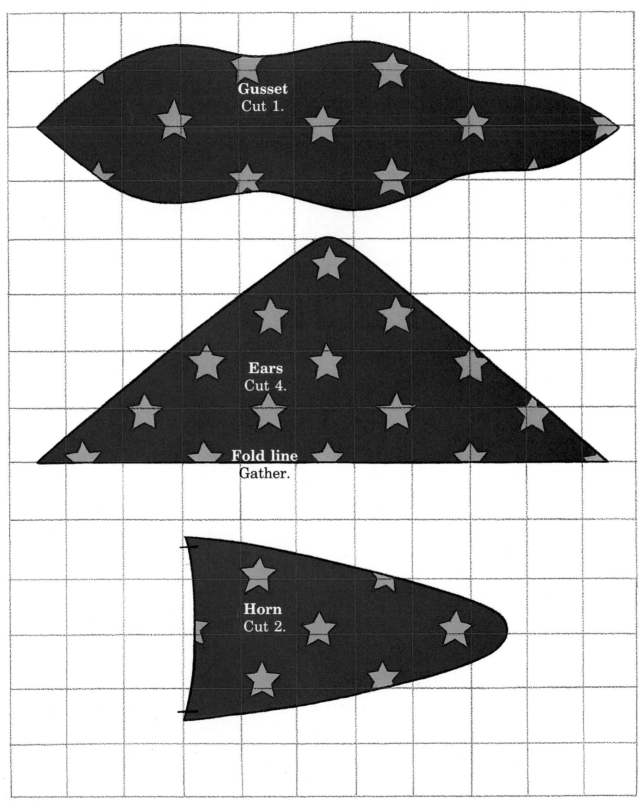

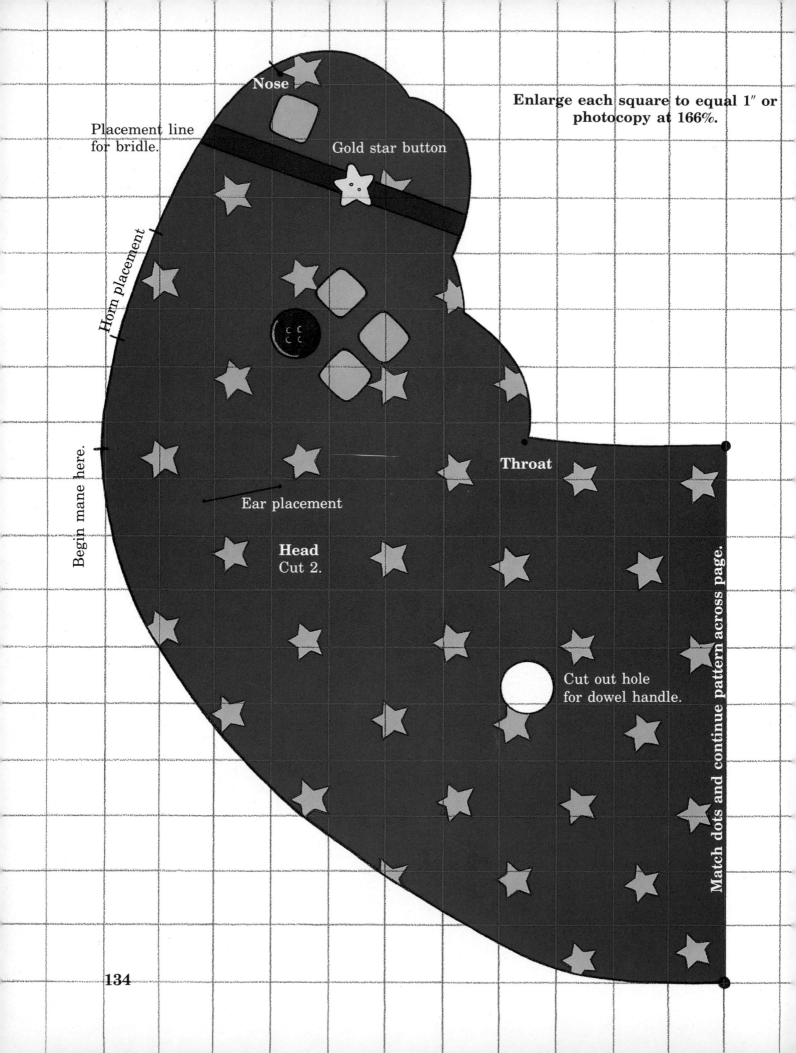

Nose

Placement line
for bridle.

Enlarge each square to equal 1″ or
photocopy at 166%.

Gold star button

Horn placement

Begin mane here.

Ear placement

Head
Cut 2.

Throat

Cut out hole
for dowel handle.

Match dots and continue pattern across page.

134

Wheel
Cut 2.

Gather on this line.

Fold line

Leave open.

Sock Critters

For a new twist on stuffed animals, combine different socks to create colorful critters, such as a star-struck cat and rabbit and a polka-dot dog. If you set up your own sock exchange with friends, you'll end up with a variety of colors and patterns from which to choose.

You will need (for 1 critter):
2 pair of adult stretch-knit novelty socks
Dressmaker's pen
Thread to match socks
Scissors
Polyester stuffing
Liquid ravel preventer
Fabric scraps for nose and cheeks
Embroidery floss in colors to contrast
   with socks
2 (¼″) black shank buttons

For the Cat:
3″ (¼″-wide) elastic
For the Rabbit:
1 skein of hot pink yarn
1 (2½″) cardboard square

Note: If your sock critter is intended for a small child, for safety's sake, use black embroidery floss to make French knot eyes instead of the buttons.

   All seam allowances are ¼″ unless otherwise noted.

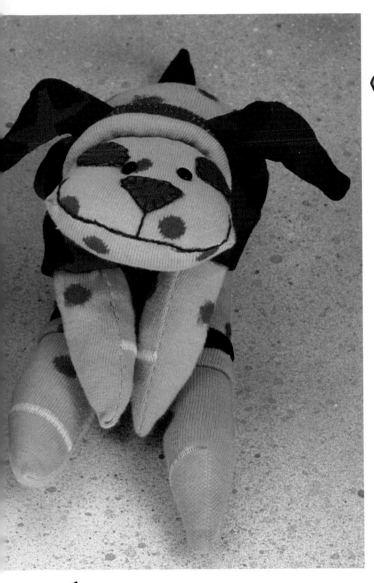

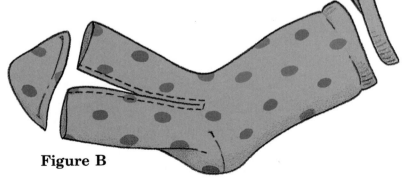

Figure A

2. To create the mouth, use 3 strands of floss to stemstitch the mouth along the seam, curving the ends up slightly in a smile. Referring to the photo, stemstitch a ⅜″ line above the center of the mouth.

Trace and cut out the nose and the cheek patterns. Transfer them to the fabric scraps and cut them out. Coat the edges with liquid ravel preventer and let them dry. Using a blanket stitch and 3 strands of floss, appliqué the nose in place above the straight center line of the mouth. Place the cheeks ½″ above the curved ends of the mouth and blanket-stitch them in place. For the eyes, sew the buttons in place just inside the lower edge of the cheeks.

3. For the jumpsuit, cut off ½″ of the top band of another sock. Then cut off the toe. Draw a line to the heel and stitch on each side of it as you did for the body, leaving the ends of the legs open. (Figure B.) Cut between the lines of stitching. For the dog and the rabbit, turn the ends of

1. To form the legs, turn 1 sock wrong side out. Beginning at the toe, draw a line on the foot of the sock up to the beginning of the heel. Leaving a 1½″ opening for turning, stitch on each side of the traced line. Cut between the lines of stitching. (Figure A.)

Cut off ½″ of the top band of the sock. Stitch the top closed to form the head, rounding the corners slightly. Turn right side out through the opening in the leg. Stuff the body firmly and slipstitch the opening closed.

Figure B

the jumpsuit legs under twice, and slip-stitch the hem in place. Turn right side out. For the cat, cut 2 (3″) strips from the scrap of the sock band. Stitch the ends together to form a circle. With right sides facing and raw edges aligned, stitch to the ends of each jumpsuit leg to form cuffs. Turn the jumpsuit right side out.

Slip the jumpsuit onto the animal. Roll the neck of the jumpsuit under 3 times, exposing the animal's face. Slipstitch the hem to the inside of the jumpsuit.

4. For the arms, use a sock the same color as the legs. Cut across the sock 5″ from the toe. Cut this piece in half lengthwise. (Figure C.) With right sides facing and raw edges aligned, stitch along the long edges. Turn. Stuff the hands firmly and lightly stuff the arms. Set aside.

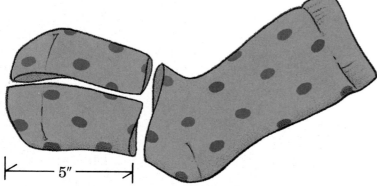

Figure C

For the sleeves, cut the toe off a contrasting sock. Then cut a 4″ piece from the foot. Cut this piece in half lengthwise. (Figure D.) With right sides facing and raw edges aligned, stitch on the long edges and turn. Fold each tube in half so wrong sides are facing and raw edges are aligned. Slip an arm into each sleeve, aligning the raw edges of both. Stitch across the end of each sleeve/arm. Repeat for the other sleeve/arm.

About 2″ down from the neck band, pinch a ¼″-deep tuck in the sides of the

jumpsuit. Insert the top raw edge of 1 sleeve/arm and slipstitch it in place. Repeat for the other sleeve/arm.

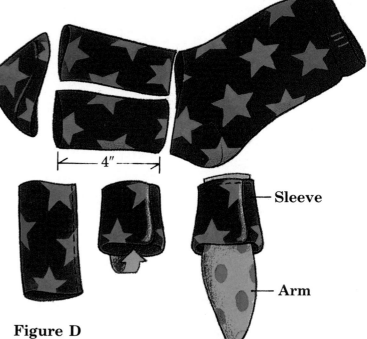

Figure D

5. For the cat's tail, cut 1 (8½″-long) section from a sock scrap; cut it in half lengthwise. With right sides facing and raw edges aligned, stitch around 1 end and along the long edges, catching the 3″ piece of elastic in the side seam to make it curl. (Figure E.) Turn and stuff the tail firmly. Make a tuck in the jumpsuit in the center of the heel in the same manner as the arms and stitch the tail in place.

Figure E

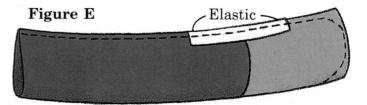

For the rabbit's tail, make a pom-pom by wrapping the yarn around the cardboard square about 100 times. Tie a doubled length of yarn through 1 end of the loops and tie it in a knot. Cut through the yarn loops on the opposite end. Fluff the tail and tack it to the jumpsuit at the center of the heel.

For the dog's tail, cut 1 (2½" x 3½") piece from a sock scrap. Fold it in half lengthwise. With right sides facing and raw edges aligned, stitch on the long raw edges and across 1 end at an angle. Trim the seam and turn the tail right side out. Center the seam on the back of the tail. Make a tuck and sew the raw end of the tail to the jumpsuit in the same manner as the arms.

6. Trace and cut out the ear pattern. Transfer the pattern to the sock scraps and cut out the ears. With right sides facing and raw edges aligned, stitch 2 ear pieces together, leaving the base open. Repeat for the other ear. Turn. For the rabbit's ears, use 3 strands of floss to blanket-stitch 1 inner ear piece to the center of each ear.

For all ears, cut 1 (3"-wide) band from the top of a sock scrap. Roll the band tightly to form a thick ring and pin edges

to secure. Make a small tuck at the center of each cat's or rabbit's ear. Slip ¼" of the end of the ears inside the pinned edges of the ring, spacing the rabbit's ears ⅛" apart, the cat's ears ½" apart, and the dog's ears 2" apart. (Figure F.) Slip-stitch the pinned edges closed, catching the ends of the ears in the seam.

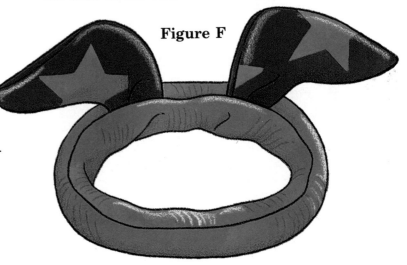

Figure F

7. Slip the ear band in place behind the neck band on the jumpsuit.

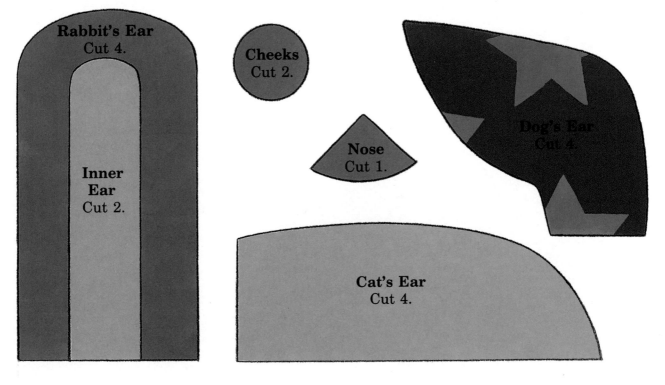

Rabbit's Ear
Cut 4.

Inner Ear
Cut 2.

Cheeks
Cut 2.

Nose
Cut 1.

Dog's Ear
Cut 4.

Cat's Ear
Cut 4.

Elephant Chair

Exploring the wilds can be exhausting work. Even a tireless adventurer may occasionally want to catch her breath, especially if she has a colorful elephant offering her a seat. With a few tools, you can create this elephant chair for the jungles in your home.

You will need:
Tracing paper
Pencil
Scissors
½ sheet of ¾″ plywood
Band saw or jigsaw
Table saw
4 small C-clamps
Tape measure or ruler
Electric drill with ¼″ and ⅝″ bits
Sandpaper: 100, 150, 180 grade
18 (1¼″-long) #8 flathead wood screws
4 (1″-long) #8 flathead wood screws
Screwdriver
Wood filler
Acrylic paints: turquoise, royal blue,
   cream, pale yellow, pink
Paintbrushes: small, medium
Black permanent marker
Acrylic matte finish
½ yard (¼″-diameter) cording

Making the Chair

1. Enlarge and cut out the pattern for the elephant. Transfer the outline of the elephant to the plywood 2 times. Then transfer the outline of the arm to the plywood 2 times.

2. Using the band saw, cut out the 2 bodies and the 2 arms. Use the table saw to cut 1 (9″ x 14″) seat, 2 (1″ x 7″) seat supports, and 2 (3″ x 14″) back slats.

3. Stack the bodies on top of each other and clamp them together with the 4 clamps. With the ¼″ bit, drill the 9 holes marked on the pattern. Be sure to drill all the way through both bodies.

4. Unclamp the bodies. Drilling from the outside of the bodies, use the ⅝″ bit to countersink the 4 back and 3 seat holes. Countersink the 2 arm holes from the inside of the bodies.

5. With the ¼″ bit, center and drill 2 holes in the seat supports, 1½″ from each end. Countersink the holes with the ⅝″ bit.

6. For the tail, make a mark in the center of the seat, ½″ from the back edge. Drill a ⅝″ hole all the way through the seat at the mark.

7. Sand all of the pieces, beginning with the coarsest grade of sandpaper and finishing with the finest.

**Assembling the Chair
(You will need a partner.)**

1. On the inside of 1 body, make a mark ⅜″ below the center of each seat hole. Draw a pencil line connecting the 3 marks. Center the top edge of 1 seat support on this line. (Figure A.) Drill 2 holes through the pre-drilled holes in the seat support into the body, being careful not to go all the way through the body. Empty the sawdust from the holes and use 2 (1¼″-long) screws to hold the support in place. Repeat for the second seat support on the inside of the other body piece.

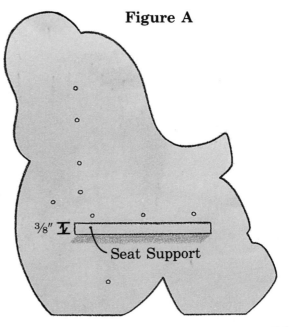

Figure A

⅜″ ⊥

Seat Support

2. On the 9″ edge of the seat, make a mark 1″ from each end and in the center. Rest the seat on a support and line up these markings with the 3 holes drilled in the body for the seat. Using the ¼″ bit, drill into the end of the seat through the pre-drilled holes. Empty the sawdust from the holes and insert 3 (1¼″-long) screws from the outside of the body into the seat. Attach the other end of the seat to the other body in the same way.

3. Postion 1 arm on the outside of 1 body. With the ¼″ bit, drill into the arm from the inside of the body through the pre-drilled holes, being careful not to go all the way through the arm. Drill the second arm in the same way. Set the arms aside for painting.

4. Referring to Figure B, draw a line on the inside of 1 body connecting the 2 upper back slat holes. Extend the line ½″ above the top hole. Connect the pair of lower holes, also extending the line ½″ above the top hole. Mark the inside of the other body in the same way.

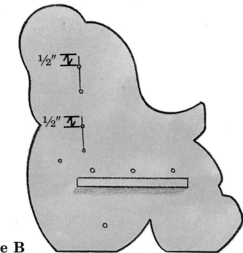

Figure B

5. Center the end of 1 back slat on 1 of the drawn lines. Align the top of the slat with the top of the line. From the outside of the body, drill through the pre-drilled holes into the slat with the ¼″ bit. Empty the sawdust from the holes. Center the remaining slat on the remaining line, with the top of the slat aligned with the top of the line. Drill through the pre-drilled holes into the slat. Drill the other end of the slats the same way.

6. Using the 1¼″-long screws, attach the back slats to the chair.

Finishing the Chair

1. Fill the countersink holes and any other holes or irregularities with wood filler. Let it dry and then sand it smooth.

2. For a base coat, paint the entire chair and arms turquoise. Let them dry.

3. Transfer the details to the outside of both bodies and to the arms. Paint the details as shown on the pattern. Allow the paint to dry; then repeat 4 or 5 times, letting the paint dry between coats.

4. Use the marker to outline the toes, socks, pants, shirt, and facial features.

5. Using a large flat brush, apply the acrylic finish to the entire chair. Let it dry; then repeat 3 times, letting it dry between coats.

6. For the tail, tie a knot in 1 end of the cording. Thread the cording through the hole in the seat and knot the other end.

7. To attach the arms, insert the 1″-long screws from the inside of the chair through the pre-drilled holes into the holes on the inside of the arms. Fill the holes with wood filler. Let the filler dry and then sand it smooth. Paint over the filler with turquoise to match the rest of the inside of the chair.

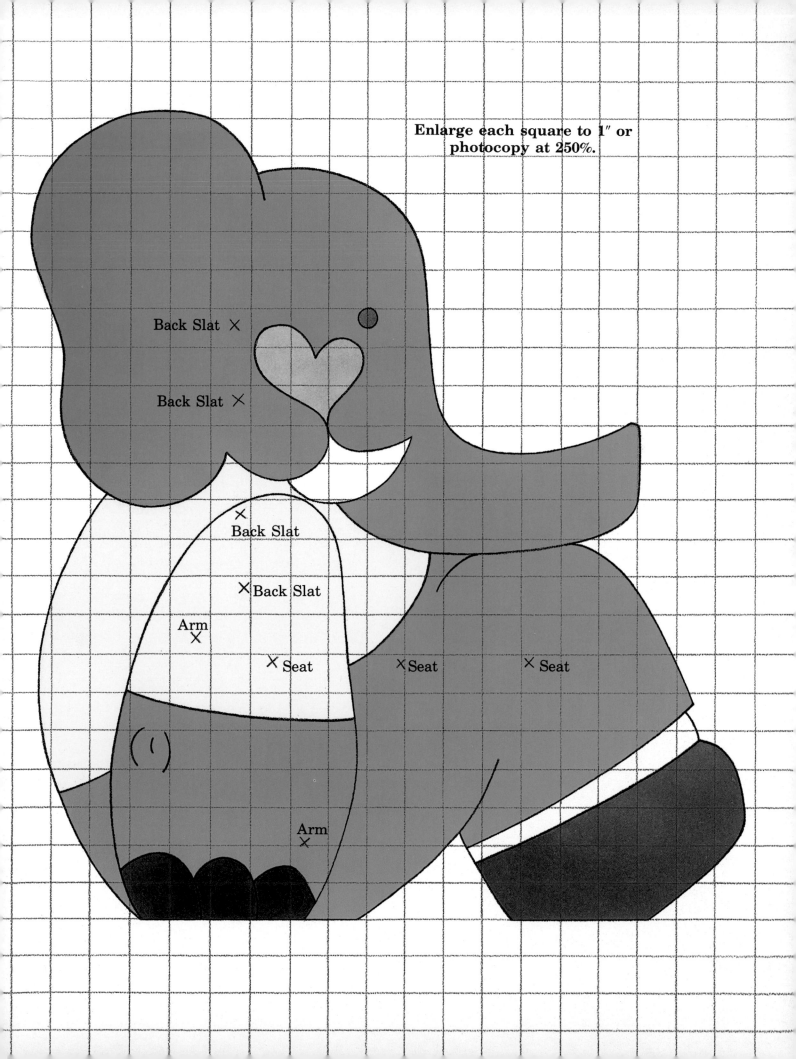

Designers & Contributors

Rina Albala, Nutty Reindeer Ornaments (concept), 58.

Kendall Boggs, Reindeer Collar, 112.

Stanhope Brasfield, Gone Fishin', 124.

Alice London Cox, Blue-ribbon Boxers, 104.

Kim Eidson Crane, Candy Garland, 40; Nutty Reindeer Ornaments, 58; Wrap It Up!, 64; Surprise Balls, 77; Decorated Dishtowels, 88; Baseball Card Catcher, 128.

Hillary Kramer Delaney, Dragon Clubhouse, 116.

Connie Formby, Mrs. Santa's Aprons, 16; North Pole Paint Set (painting), 32; Stardust Wands, 34; Gone Fishin' (painting), 124.

Linda Hendrickson, Greetings from Santa, 68; Mailbox Cover, 70; St. Nick Apron, 96; Belly Bags, 106; A Magical Mount, 130; Sock Critters, 136; Elephant Chair, 140.

Eve London, Glitter Ornaments (Glitter Sticks), 48.

Charlotte Lyons, Fleecy Sweats, 99.

L. Amanda Owens, Novelty Knits, 110.

Jonathan Peat, Squish 'n Wish, 92.

Janet A. Rubino, Oodles of Noodles, 45.

Betsy Scott, Christmas Tree Skirt, 42; Bank on It, 85; Tags to Go, 86.

Linda Martin Stewart, Glitter Ornaments (Star Brights, Sticky-Star Balls), 48; Holiday Doorkeepers, 51; Spoon Angel, 67; Refrigerator Magnets, 78; Key Holder, 82; Paperwhites, 90.

Elizabeth Taliaferro, Mrs. Santa's Christmas Cottage, 8; Peppermint Skates, 20; Prancer's Peanut Butter Dough, 26; Reindeer Games, 28; Bubblegum Baubles, 30; North Pole Paint Set (recipe), 32; Stardust Wands (recipe), 34; Santa's Dominoes, 37.

Carol M. Tipton, Animal Zoobilee, 60.

DeeDee Triplett, Ribbon Candy, 56.

Emilie White, Crazy Hats (red), 74.

Madeline O'Brien White, Crazy Hats, 74.

Special thanks to **Lowell Baltzell, Linda Keller and Barkley,** and the following shops in Birmingham, Alabama for sharing their resources with *Christmas is Coming!*: **Applause Dancewear & Accessories; Chocolate Soup, Inc., Huffstutler's Hardware Home Center; Jack N' Jill Shop; Sikes Children's Shoes; Vestavia Hills Apothecary.**